WOMEN
of the
BIBLE
Tell All

Opal Ashenbrenner

ISBN: 1456433776
ISBN-13: 9781456433772
Library of Congress Control Number: 2010918381
CreateSpace, North Charleston, SC

ACKNOWLEDGMENTS

My heartfelt thanks to those special people in my life who have inspired, encouraged, and supported me as this manuscript came together. I love you all.

To Donald the love of my life, whose unconditional love gave me courage to dare to fulfill my dreams.

To good friend, Judy McKee who sparked the idea of the interviews when she interviewed me as Sarah in our recent Bible study. Thank you Judy and Kenneth for the memories of the wonderful trips the four of us shared and for being the ones I call on when I have a need.

To Maurine Ross, my prayer and accountability partner, for believing in me and convincing me God has a purpose in these interviews. Thank you for your support, encouragement, prayers, proofreading skills, and for keeping me Biblically correct. A special thank you to Bob who helped with the chapter titles.

To the Sisters of Sara Sunday School Class, a wonderful group of women who were the first to preview the interviews and offer encouragement and support. Thank you for your love and for allowing me to be your part-time Bible teacher.

To my wonderful children and grandchildren who never fail to overwhelm me with their love and devotion. A special thanks to grandchildren, Brian and Kelly for their help in seeing this manuscript come together.

Thank you Brian for the photograph on the book's cover of my two beautiful granddaughters, Brooke and Kelly. Thank you Kelly for your editorial skills and suggestions. I couldn't have done it without you.

Most of all, I thank my Lord and Savior Jesus Christ for His continued blessings.

INTRODUCTION

As I began to look deeper into the lives of these women of the Bible, I began to wonder about their feelings. As you discuss the questions at the end of each interview, perhaps you will discover thoughts and feeling you have in common with these extraordinary women. These interviews are not meant to add to or take away from the words of the Bible, only to make the women more real by probing the feelings behind the stories. In these stories, we see their humanity. We also see how much God loved and cared for them, sometimes in spite of themselves. These interviews are stories of love and devotion—of faith lost and found. They touch our hearts and compel us to reflect on the place of Biblical truths in our busy daily lives. None of the women we have interviewed was perfect. Their flaws, failures, and sins are exposed as examples for us. The sins of these women and others recorded in the Bible do not in any way mean that we are to glorify their wrongdoing. Sin is exposed to remind us of our sin, and give us comfort that God can use imperfect people to accomplish His purpose. What He did in the lives of these thirty-four outstanding women, He is still doing in the lives of every true believer today. As with these women, you have a unique and wonderful destiny that God has planned with you alone in mind.

This book is fiction based on true stories in the Bible. All scriptures quoted are from the New International Version.

TABLE OF CONTENTS

SECTION ONE

WOMEN OF THE OLD TESTAMENT

"You spread out our sins before you—our secret sins— and you see them all."

PSALM 90:8 NLT

THE STORY OF
ADAM'S PRIME RIB (EVE)
GENESIS 2–4

We know little about our guest for today, even though she has been called "The Mother of All Living." She is the final piece in the creation story. After creating man and placing him in the garden, God decided man needed another human being with whom to fellowship. Adam needed someone like himself, yet different enough for a relationship in order to populate the earth. God could have made woman from the dust of the ground as He did man; however, He chose to make her from man's flesh and bone. We are fortunate to have that woman with us today. Eve, can you tell us what you were thinking when you opened your eyes for the very first time.

I felt and heard my eternal God for the first time, and somehow I knew I had been created to glorify, worship, and praise Him! Then God gave me to Adam, and I felt complete. Adam was different from me. I liked what I saw, and he seemed pleased with me.

There in the Garden of Eden, God spoke, and the institution of marriage began. Man and woman were symbolically united as one for God declared, "For this reason a man will leave his father and mother, and be united to his wife, and they will become one flesh." That must have been a beautiful ceremony.   Most modern day weddings are patterned after the first ceremony. God was the ultimate Wedding Planner.

My wedding was awesome. I did not have to worry about bridesmaids, reception, or any of the details that plague most weddings. God gave us to each other to love and enjoy and our lives were perfect. He placed us in a beautiful garden, and gave us a free will to do as we pleased.

You were the first and only woman on earth at this time. You were the first wife, the first mother, the first grandmother, and ultimately, the first sinner. You were living in a perfect world with no problems. The best part was your personal relationship with God. Eve, If the garden was so beautiful, and everything was perfect, how can you explain the tragedy we know as the fall of humankind?

I cannot explain it. I do not t know how it happened. I guess I was an easy target. My life was perfect, and I never dreamed it could be any other way. One day as I was playing with the baby animals, the serpent spoke to me. He asked if God really had told us we could eat of all the fruit in the garden. I assured him God had said we could eat from any of the fruit except the fruit from the tree in the center of the garden. I explained to the serpent God said if we ate of the fruit of that tree, we would surely die.

The serpent was very clever, wasn't he? Even as he does today, he set out to get you to doubt God. He implied God was strict, stingy, and selfish for not wanting you to share in the knowledge of good and evil. He said you wouldn't die, but your eyes would be opened, and you would become like God. You would know everything! The serpent saw you were interested, and true to form, he went on to promise you would gain new understanding and wisdom.

I am not making excuses for my sin; however, I did not have any role model or mentor to help me. I had no experience with deceit or wrongdoing, so the serpent easily convinced me it was not wrong, just different. He asked why I would not want to escape from this garden and be my own person. He convinced me God would not be angry with me for wanting to be my own person. That sounded right to me, so I allowed myself to be convinced. I wondered what it would be like to make my own decisions.

We know the rest of the story. You were focusing on the one thing you could not have, and forgetting the good things God had given you. Not only did you eat the fruit from the forbidden tree, but also you gave some to Adam. What happened then?

Instantly our eyes were opened and we realized we had done wrong. When we heard the Lord God walking in the garden, we hid from Him among the trees because we were afraid. We realized for the first time we were naked, so we sewed fig leaves together and tried to make coverings to hide our nakedness.

I can understand you were afraid when you heard God calling you that evening. You confessed you had eaten of the tree, and Adam blamed you for giving him the fruit to eat. When asked how you could do such a thing, you told God the serpent had tricked you. God immediately placed a curse on the serpent that he would grovel in the dust and crawl on his belly as long as he lived. God also gave the first prophecy that Satan's offspring and your offspring would be enemies and your offspring would crush the head of Satan's offspring. I believe He also had a few choice words for you and Adam.

Yes, He did. It broke my heart to hear the consequences of our sin. God said I would bear children with intense pain and suffering. He said Adam would have to work for a living. In addition, he would have to sweat to produce food all his days, and one day we would die. God said we had to leave the beautiful Garden of Eden. However, before banishing us from the garden, God sewed animal skins together to make clothing for us. I took that as a sign that He still loved us in spite of our sin. Oh, why did I listen to that serpent?

* * *

Many a sinner has cried that same thing. Eve found that God's wrath is real, but His grace is abundant. Eve was the first sinner, but she was also the first to receive God's grace. By His grace, Eve was forgiven, and her relationship with God was restored. She had children, though she suffered pain in childbirth and heartache in parenting. Amid Eve's pain over the loss of Abel, she conceived another son, Seth. He lived a godly life, and through his lineage, Jesus Christ was born into the world.

THOUGHTS FOR DISCUSSION FROM THE LIFE OF EVE

- Scripture tells us that Adam was created in the image of God. What does it mean to be made in the image of God?

- Satan tempted Eve with doubt that God meant what He said. Do you ever doubt that God means what He says when your prayers are not answered immediately? How do you deal with doubt?

- In what ways do people deceive themselves when they try to justify being disobedient to God?

- Eve blamed the serpent for her sin, and Adam blamed Eve. Do we ever try to blame others for our sins? Have you ever done this and then been found out? How did you feel?

- What was the significance of God sewing animal skins to cover their sin?

- Do we realize that when we open ourselves to sin, we are also opening ourselves for God's wrath? How was Eve's relationship with God altered after she sinned?

- What was the hope that God gave Eve after she sinned? How was that hope kept alive?

- When will that hope be fulfilled completely?

GOD'S BEAUTIFUL
PRINCESS (SARAH)
GENESIS 12:10-20;
16:1-15; 21:1-10

I am sure most of you have heard of our guest today. She is mentioned fifty three times in the Bible; more than any other woman. She was given the name of Sarai at birth. Welcome Sarai. Sarai is a very beautiful and unusual name. Will you tell us how you came to be named Sarai?

Sarai was the name of the devotees of Ningal, the moon god worshipped in my native Assyria. The Assyrian meaning of Sarai is argumentative. My husband would probably agree that meaning fits me perfectly. I prefer the Hebrew meaning of Sarai, which is princess.

I can understand why you felt like a princess. You and Abram were living a life of luxury in Ur, a sophisticated society. You were treated like a princess. What did you think when your husband informed you God said he would be the father of a great nation, and you should leave the land of Ur and go to an unnamed land?

Since I was barren, I wondered how Abram would father a child. I wasn't happy about leaving the lifestyle I enjoyed in Ur. However, I had to go with my husband because that is what wives did in my day. I am sure I whined a lot on the way. I told him more than once I thought he was out of his mind. I was sure God must have meant Caesarea, not Canaan. I tried to get him to pray about it a few days, but he was determined. I wanted to be an obedient wife, so I went. I was a believer in God, and I did believe He would take care of us.

When you arrived in Canaan, you found the country in a severe drought. Abram decided you should go to Egypt to wait out the famine.

I begged him to go back home, but he would not listen. Therefore, we traveled on to Egypt. Before we arrived there, Abram became afraid the Egyptians might take me because I was a beautiful woman.

Abram came up with a plan to tell the Egyptians you were his sister. It was not a complete lie. You and Abram had the same father, but different mothers. That made you Abram's half sister. Sarai, why did you go along with his plan?

I was torn, but I did go along with his plan. When he first mentioned his plan, I wondered if I was less valuable to him because I not been able to give him a son. I was disappointed in my husband for making such a proposal; however, I could see the wisdom of his plan, and I was getting tired of the nomadic life.

When you arrived in Egypt, Abram's fears were justified. The palace officials saw you and sang your praises to the Pharaoh. The Pharaoh ordered you brought to his harem. He gave Abram many gifts because of you.

I was afraid of being in a harem; however, I did trust God and prayed for His protection. Soon, God sent a terrible plague upon Pharaoh's household. Realizing the plagues were because he had brought me into his household, the Pharaoh rebuked

Abram sharply. He gave Abram some sheep and camels, and ordered him to take me and leave. You can bet we beat a hasty retreat. I know you are dying to know, so I will tell you. No, I did not sleep with the Pharaoh!

Sarai, we know your biggest disappointment in life was that you were childless. You were fearful you would never have a child, and the covenant God had made with Abram would not be fulfilled. You decided it was time to help God keep His promise. I know you don't know Dr. Phil, but to borrow a couple of questions from him; "What in the world were you thinking?" and "How did that work for you?"

I was seventy-five years of age, and I did not see how I could give my husband a son. I knew God had promised Abram he would be the father of a great nation. My husband had waited a long time, so I decided to give God a hand. I began looking for a surrogate. It was a tough decision. Would I choose one that was beautiful or unattractive? My first thought was to pick the ugliest, puniest woman I could find. I did want a healthy son, so I picked this young, healthy Gentile handmaiden. I told Abram about my plan, and he was all for it. You know how men are! As to how that worked for me, it was extremely difficult those nights she went in to sleep with my husband. It worked well for awhile after the baby was born. I had a baby to cuddle; however, as he grew it became increasingly difficult. I began to wonder myself what I was thinking. I thought I was doing the right thing at the time; however, I soon came to realize how foolish I was. God did not need my help. My decision to pick a Gentile maid was another mistake. By picking Hagar instead of a handmaiden from my own tribe created a conflict that has escalated over centuries.

Sarai, you are a good example that God never gives up on us, in spite of our sin. When Abram was ninety-nine years old, the Lord renewed the covenant He made earlier. At this time, God changed Abram's name to Abraham, and promised to give him a son. You were listening from the tent nearby and heard that promise. What did you think?

I did not think anyone would know I was listening. By then I was ninety years old, and the thought of me carrying a child for nine months and going through childbirth made me laugh.

Sarai, you had been waiting all these years to have a child, so we can understand why it was hard for you to believe what you were hearing. I do not think you laughed from a lack of faith in what God could do, but from doubt about what He could do through you. When confronted about your laughter, you lied.

I had trusted and waited all this time, and had lost hope. Then to hear God's servant say that I would have a son was unreal. I laughed and cried at the same time. What an amazing example of grace that God did not punish me for lying. He just continued to bless us with the birth of my son a year later. God changed my hated name of Sarai to Sarah. Maybe now, God thought I had matured enough to be called princess.

I'm sure you were quite mature by this time. Isaac grew, and one day God commanded Abraham to take Isaac to Mount Moriah. Sarah, did you have any idea what Abraham had in mind that day?

My husband did not tell me, but I knew something was up. If I had known what he had in mind, I might have reverted to being Sarai that day! However, by now I had learned to trust my husband and my God. Life is so much easier that way.

9

Sarah, you truly are a remarkable woman, and you lived an extraordinary life. If I decide to write your life story, what would you want people to know about you?

I want people to know that God did not give up on me, even though I became impatient and thought I would help Him keep His promise to Abraham. I made many wrong decisions centuries ago, and people today are living with the consequences. God still loved me and blessed me. I think I would like to be remembered as a sinner saved by the grace of God.

* * *

We know the rest of Sarah's story. We know of the conflict with her Egyptian handmaiden, and on some level, we can all identify with her feelings. We see the problems created when we try to help God accomplish His purposes in our lives. We can learn from Sara's life that God responds to faith even in the midst of failure. God changed Sarah's heart. It took ninety years for Sarah to become "God's Princess." What will it take for us?

THOUGHTS FOR DISCUSSION
FROM THE LIFE OF SARAH

- What valid arguments could Sarah have given when Abraham said they were to go to an unknown land?

- There came a time when Abraham asked Sarah to lie about their relationship. Do you consider a half-truth a sin? Why or why not?

- When the Pharaoh discovered the truth, do you think God acted not to punish Abraham for lying, but to protect Sarah from assault? Give reasons for your answer.

- How difficult is it to trust God when you think His promise is humanly impossible? Do you find it hard to believe in miracles? Have you ever experienced a miracle?

- What do you believe to be God's motive for delaying His answer to Sarah and Abraham's prayer for a child?

- How did Sarah justify rushing ahead of God?

- How far should a wife go to help her husband fulfill what God has called him to do?

- What was the significance of God changing her name from Sarai to Sarah and Abram's to Abraham?

- What was Abraham's intention when he took Isaac to Mount Moriah? Why did God ask Abraham to make such a sacrifice?

- Which of these words do you think best describes Sarah - Submissive, obedient, manipulative, impatient, selfish, disobedient, mean-spirited, and repentant? Explain your answer. Can you think of other descriptive words?

- What is the legacy that Sarah leaves that we are still living with today?

ONE OF THE LEAST OF THESE (HAGAR)
GENESIS 16:1–15; 21:1–21

In the midst of the great story about Abraham and Sarah, we must not overlook the story of Hagar. Hagar is with us today to share her story. What was your life like as a slave to such an important Jewish couple?

My life was not easy. I was taken from my home in Egypt, and brought to Canaan as a slave. As a slave, I was subject to my owner's every whim. My only value to my owners was in providing labor or having children.

Hagar, your story places you in the very center of Israel's history. What was your reaction when the wife of the owner asked you to sleep with her husband to give her a child? How did you feel about being a surrogate mother?

Of course, I was thrilled. I knew of my master's wife's inability to have a child, so I felt I would be treated very well. Sarai had shared with me that God had promised her husband his heirs would be as numerous as the stars in the sky. She was getting old, and did not think she would ever have a child. Abram was a good man. He was always kind to me, so I thought it would not be too bad. Anything would be better than being a slave.

13

You probably did not have much choice in the matter. Hagar, when you knew you were pregnant, you began to despise Sarai. What happened then?

It was great at first. After awhile she began to get on my nerves, telling me what to do, what to eat, and how to act around her husband. I will have to admit I got a little snippy with her occasionally. She became so overbearing and hateful that I finally ran away. Then the angel of the Lord found me and told me to go back to Sarai and submit to her. He promised that God would increase my descendants so they would be too numerous to count.

You went back and were submissive to Sarai. You had a son, and Abram gave him the name Ishmael. How did that work out for you this time?

She treated me better for a while after my baby was born. She was happy to have a baby to cuddle and love. I soon came to despise her. This was my baby, and I should have been the one to cuddle and love him. Therefore, it did cause trouble between us. Maybe I did taunt her a little about not being able to have a child. However, it was her jealous and better-than-thou attitude that caused our problems.

Eventually, God blessed Abraham and Sarah with a child of their own. As the boys grew, Sarah became afraid your child would lay claim to all or part of Isaac's inheritance. At this time, disagreements began to escalate between the two of you, and Sarah demanded Abraham make you and your son leave their household. That must have been very hard for you. Abraham gave in to his wife, and asked you to leave. I am sure Abraham was very sorry to see you go.

I did feel a little sorry for him. He really did love our son, and I like to think he had some feelings for me. Ishmael was his own flesh and blood and I felt a part of his heart would leave with us.

Nevertheless, leave you did. God may not have approved of Sarah's hateful plan, but He allowed it. I can just imagine the old man's brokenness as he gave you food and water and sent you off with the boy. I am sure there were tears in his eyes as he watched you leave, knowing he would probably never see his son again. I cannot even imagine the heartache he must have felt.

I will give him that. He helped us prepare for the journey by giving us food and water. However, he did not offer to send a servant to go with us for protection.

Where did you and Ishmael go from there?

We went on our way and wandered around in the desert of Beersheba. I felt lost and alone. I had no idea where I was going or what I was going to do. After days of wandering around, our food and water was gone. Do you know how it is to have your child begging for food, and you have none to give him? I thought we were going to die. His cries broke my heart. I could not watch my son die, so I kissed him goodbye, and walked a few feet away to await my own death.

I cannot even imagine how you suffered at that moment. No one loves like a mother, and you were in an impossible situation. Then an amazing thing happened. Scripture tells us that God heard the boy crying. Did Ishmael cry because he was afraid or in pain, or because he could hear his mother

sobbing? God heard the sobs of you and your son as if they were prayers without words and He answered as He always does when we cry out to Him

At that moment, an angel of God appeared and assured me God heard our cries. He said that I should not be afraid, but to go and comfort my son. Then He gave me a great promise. He said, "I will make a great nation from this boy's descendants."

This was the first appearance of an angel in the Scriptures. How that must have encouraged you. Scripture tells us that God then opened your eyes and you saw a well of water. God had saved the life of you and your child by bringing water to you. Can you tell us about your life after this?

God was with my son and he grew up to become an expert archer. I arranged a marriage for him with a young woman from my native Egypt, and God made his descendants into a great nation.

* * *

Genesis 16:13 says, "Hagar referred to the Lord, who had spoken to her, as "the God who sees me," for she said, "I have seen the One who sees me!" Therefore, we can assume Hagar came to know the Lord. WHAT HAPPENED TO ISHMAEL? Ishmael had twelve sons (same as Abraham), and these sons have become leaders of the Arab tribes and Muslim religion. Another interesting fact and Jewish tie to the Arab nation was that Esau married the daughter of Ishmael (Gen. 28:9). There always has been, and always will be, trouble between the Arabs and God's chosen people. It began with our story of Sarah and Hagar and escalated through the ages.

* * *

Have you ever noticed how God's plan incorporates people's mistakes? God used Hagar and Ishmael even though there was sin in their lives. Their story reminds us that every person has value in God's sight. God had a plan for Ishmael, as well as the son of promise, Isaac. It is amazing how God always provides for His own if His children cry out for help.

THOUGHTS FOR DISCUSSION FROM THE LIFE OF HAGAR

- Hagar was a slave and did not have much choice about her situation. Even in difficult situations, we have a choice about our attitude. What was Hagar's attitude toward her childless mistress?

- Even though it was Sarah's plan for Hagar to bear Abraham's child, what was her attitude toward Hagar after the baby was born?

- We feel sorry for Hagar when she and her son were cast out because of Sarah's jealously. What evidence do we see that God was watching over her?

- How difficult would it have been for Hagar to go back to her mistress in obedience to the commandment of the angel? What sort of reception did she receive from Sarah when she went back?

- How do you explain God's care for Hagar and her son?

- From Hagar's story, we can learn that God is faithful to His plan and promises, even when humans complicate the process. Can you think of a time when you have complicated the process and God continued to bless? Explain what you learned.

- We know Hagar was a woman found by God, heard by God, seen by God, and loved by God. Share your story of how you were found by God, seen by God, and loved by God.

THE MOTHER WHO LOVED
TOO MUCH (REBEKAH)
GENESIS 24:1-67; 27:1-40

The story of Rebekah our guest for today really begins with Abraham. Abraham was afraid his son might marry one of the pagan Canaanite women, so he sent his trusted servant to the hometown of his uncle Nahor to find a wife for Isaac. This was a common practice of the day in order for the lineage to remain pure. Eliezer the servant was old and his journey was long and hard. He reached the village where Abraham's relatives lived, and came to rest at the well in the village. Rebekah, please share with us your thoughts when you first saw this elderly man sitting there at the well.

It was eventide, the usual time for the women of the town to come and draw water. As I drew my water, I became aware of the old man sitting at the well praying. Obviously, he was a stranger from far away, who stood by with ten thirsty camels. He looked at me and asked for a drink of water. The custom of the day was that women at the well would offer water to weary travelers. Because he was elderly, and looked so weary, I felt sorry for him. After I had given him water to drink, I offered to draw water for his camels. I made several trips to the well drawing water for his camels until they all had enough to drink.

That must have seemed a bit unusual for him to stand there praying while you drew water for his camels. However, you found out later he had been asking God to help him accomplish the purpose of his journey. He was asking God for a sign that would help him know when he had found the right woman. He was not looking for physical beauty, though you were a very beautiful young woman. He was looking for a young woman with an attitude of service. Your offer to water his camels, in addition to giving him a drink of water, indicated to him he had found in you that kind of attitude. You were an answer to his prayer almost before he finished praying. So tell us what happened next.

When the camels finished drinking, the man asked about my family. I told him I was the daughter of Bethuel and the granddaughter of Nahor. The servant fell down and began worshiping the Lord. To make a long story short, I took him to my home, and my brother and father went out to meet him. They decided I should go with the servant to Canaan and become the bride of his son, Isaac. It was a long journey; however, as soon as I saw Isaac, my future husband, I fell in love. It seemed he felt the same way, so we were married.

Your marriage to Isaac must have been a good one since it was the first monogamous marriage on record. Though blessed with the love of your husband, your one heartache was that God had not blessed you with children. For twenty years, you longed for a child. You and Isaac must have loved each other very much, because you did not succumb to the tradition of the day, and give him your handmaiden to produce a child. Isaac loved you and prayed to the only one who could remedy the situation. Scripture tells us, "Isaac prayed to the Lord on behalf of his wife because she was barren." Rebekah, tell us what happened then.

After twenty years, God answered Isaac's prayer and I became pregnant. It was not an easy pregnancy, and I panicked. I went to the Lord and asked why this was happening to me. He told me that two nations were in my womb, and there would be a lifelong struggle between their descendants. I could not believe it when I found out there were two children in my womb. I did not understand all God was telling me then, but when my boys were born, I could see they were quite different. I suppose Isaac and I were not very wise parents. Isaac favored Esau the older son because he was bold, daring, strong, and was a hunter. I, on the other hand, was drawn to Jacob because he had a gentle, caring nature and was more like me.

I am sure raising sons with very different personalities was an uncommon challenge. We all make mistakes raising our children; however, your favoritism manifested itself in different ways, which ultimately ended up with dire circumstances. Rebekah, what were you thinking? How could you favor one child over another?

I don't know. Maybe I was destined to favor the younger one. He was my baby and God had revealed to me while they were still in the womb that the older would serve the younger. Because of that prophecy, I felt I had to do all I could to see that it came true. From the time they were small, I began treating Jacob as the leader he was to become. As they grew older, Esau was always out somewhere hunting or doing heaven knows what, but Jacob was always by my side. Then one day Esau thought so carelessly of his birthright that he sold it to Jacob for a pot of stew. I thought this was just a confirmation that my Jacob was to be the one to receive his father's blessing and the prosperity, power, and blessings of God that belonged to him.

Rebekah, I no longer see you as the innocent young girl standing by the town well with a clay jar perched on your shoulder, but a manipulative mother determined to see your favorite son inherit all God intended no matter who you hurt. You taught Jacob to make the stew that Esau wanted so badly that he sold Jacob his birthright. Then, as your husband became old and blind, and you knew he was about to die, you were determined that Jacob would receive his last blessing even though it was meant for the oldest son.

Sometimes we set in motion things we cannot take back. That is what happened here. Esau went hunting and I saw the opportunity for Jacob to receive the last blessing. Jacob was a little hesitant, and wanted to know what would happen if his father was not fooled by my plan and would call a curse down on him. I was afraid he was going to back out of the plan, so I told him to let the curse fall on me. I was willing to give up everything for my son. Isn't that what mothers do?

Rebekah, you loved much, but unwisely. Obviously, your plan worked and Jacob did receive the blessing intended for the older brother, Esau. However, in doing so, a rift was created between the two boys, and Esau threatened to kill his brother.

I think I was just beginning to see what I had done, but as is so often the case, it was too late. There was no going back. After hearing Esau's threat, I knew Jacob had to get away, so I had to do something. His father was old and sick, and it did not take much to convince him that Jacob should go to my brother Laban in Haran to find a wife. It broke my heart to see him go. I never saw my youngest son again.

Rebekah, my heart goes out to you because you finally learned that sin has consequences. Not only did you never see your favorite son again, but I'm sure your last days were not happy having to live with your other son, Esau, who would always remember his mother's part in deceiving him.

* * *

Scripture tells us that Esau learned that his father blessed Jacob, and did not have a blessing for him, he wept. Isaac told him he would live by the sword and would serve his brother. We can see why Esau wept, but we can't condone his next actions. When Esau realized how displeasing the Canaanite women he had married were to his father and mother, he left and took as his next wife, the daughter of Ishmael. Wonder how that worked out for all of them?

THOUGHTS FOR DISCUSSION
FROM THE LIFE OF REBEKAH

- What is the danger of having favorites among our children?

- Does the end ever justify the means? Choose sides and debate the question.

- On whose behalf did she deceive her husband; the Lord's, her son Jacob's, or her own? Make a case for any or for all three.

- She knew her sons' personalities and weaknesses. Maybe she could not picture Esau as leader of their people. Was she justified in taking matters into her own hands?

- Could Isaac have just pretended to be tricked, or was he, too aware of the different personalities of the boys?

- How might she have handled the situation so the outcome would have been different?

- What were Rebekah's redeeming qualities?

- Although we might not plan as elaborate a deception as Rebekah's, what are some more subtle ways we intentionally deceive other people?

- What was the significance of Esau marrying into Ishmael's tribe?

A NEGLECTED WOMAN IN
THE BIBLE (TAMAR)
GENESIS 38:1–30

The events surrounding the life of our guest for today are confusing and somewhat upsetting. Her story may be more fitting for Jerry Springer or Oprah's show; however, the story of Tamar, a neglected woman in the Bible, has a message for us. Let us not be so quick to judge this brave woman without looking at the laws of the day. The story of Tamar is one of the Bible's best examples of the Levirate marriage law in ancient Israel. This was the ancient custom of marriage between a man and the widow of his brother required by the Mosaic Law when no child was born before the man's death. Tamar, would you tell us how this law affected your marriage?

It was an arranged marriage as most marriages were in my day. I had no choice in the matter. Judah, the patriarch of his family, arranged a marriage between myself and Err, his oldest son. My husband was a wicked man, so the Lord took his life before we could have any children. Widows in those days could not inherit a husband's property and had no means of support. However, the Levirate marriage law declares when a married man dies, his closest male relative must marry the widow in order to produce an heir for the deceased man's estate. Following that law, Judah turned me over to his second son. This may sound strange to you, but we were living in a world where women had no rights, so handing me off to the next son, Oman, would at least ensure some security.

Then I understand God also took Oman's life because he did not want to have a child with his brother's widow. So again, you were left a widow.

I had no rights as a widow, so Judah told me to go back to my father's house. He said I should remain a widow until his youngest son was old enough to marry me. I was sure he would never allow me to marry his third son for fear this one would die. I had no choice but to go back to my father's house.

Tamar, you had endured a succession of funerals and husbands, and now you were sent back home. Your story was not unusual; it was typical of the culture of the day. A woman's most important function was bearing children, who would perpetuate the family line. The third son grew up, and you were not called to marry him. You decided to take matters into your own hands. It must have taken a great deal of courage for someone in your position. Can you tell us what you did?

Several years had passed, and I heard the wife of my former father-in-law had died. After the mourning period was over, Judah came to Timnah to supervise the shearing of his sheep. I took off my mourning clothes, put on a veil so I would not be recognized, and sat at the gate. Judah noticed me and thought I was a prostitute. We haggled over a price and finally agreed on one young goat, which I knew was the going rate of the day for a prostitute. However, having dealt with Judah before, I knew how dishonest he could be, so I asked for some collateral. I asked him to leave his signet ring, belt, and staff with me until he paid me with the goat.

A few days later, Judah's friend showed up with the goat to pay the harlot. When the friend could not find the harlot, I am sure Judah was willing to forget about the whole affair, including the ring and staff. Tamar, you were smart; you waited until the time was right to go to him.

Several months later, Judah heard his ex-daughter-in-law was pregnant. I am sure he was furious. After all, he was a leader of God's holy people in Israel, a patriarch of the church, and the family through which God planned to bless all the families of the world. He just could not have his daughter-in-law embarrassing the family name. He sent his people after me with the idea that I would be burned to death for my sin according to the law of the day.

Ignoring his own sin, Judah was coming down hard on you. He ordered, "Bring her out and burn her!" Tamar, you sent a message to your father-in-law. What did you say to him?

I said the man who owns this seal and walking stick is the father of my child. I asked if he recognized them. Judah immediately recognized these things as his, and realized what had happened. He said, "She hath been more righteous than I; because I gave her not to Selah my son." He did admit he had not allowed me to marry his youngest son; however, he did not take responsibility for the way he had treated me.

At least, you were finally vindicated. You bore Judah twins, and the dynasty of Judah would continue. There would be a future where once there was none, even if it would not be the respectable way Judah intended. You are a very strong woman, Tamar. While we cannot condone your methods, we cannot help but admire the way you stood up for yourself.

You chose to adhere to your faith, and take matters into your own hands to follow the law. I do not know if you were aware of God's control, but I do know that His will was accomplished. Without your daring actions, the line of Judah may have ceased to exist.

* * *

Why do we need to hear Tamar's story? Her story is embarrassing and does not mention God, except as the one who killed Tamar's first two husbands. We need to hear her story because the first book of the New Testament places her in the genealogy of our Savior.

THOUGHTS FOR DISCUSSION
FROM THE LIFE OF TAMAR

- What do you think is the purpose of Tamar's story?

- Do you think Tamar was out of line for demanding her rights? How could she have handled things differently?

- Tell of a time in your life when you were bold in your convictions, discipleship, and willingness and risked stepping out of your respectability in order to be faithful to God.

- Discuss the statement - The sins we try to cover up are the ones that anger us most when we see them in others. Give the example in this story.

- Have you ever been in a situation where you were unjustly treated? Describe the event and your personal reaction to it. What did you do about it?

- Do you see Tamar as a seductress or survivor? Defend your answer.

- Where does Tamar fit in the ancestral line of our Lord and Savior, Jesus Christ?

BEAUTIFUL IN GOD'S
EYES (LEAH)
GENESIS 29:1-35; 30:1-55

Our visitor today is a woman of incredible bravery. She is a woman, unloved, rejected, and made to feel worthless by those who should have loved her. Her story is also one of God's protection and care. Her gentle and submissive spirit kept her from becoming bitter or arrogant in a difficult situation. Leah's courageous testimony reflects her inner beauty. Leah, will you us a little about your family?

My father, Laban, was a wealthy sheep breeder. He was self-centered, controlling, manipulative, and at times abusive. My younger sister was very beautiful and was favored by our father and all who knew her. I, on the other hand am homely with weak eyes. I felt my father resented me because I was the older one and no one had wanted to marry me.

Leah, you are selling yourself short. You have beautiful eyes, and your demeanor makes you a lovely person. Your story involves your sister Rachel who found the love of her life. You couldn't help being just a little jealous, could you?

I will have to admit I was jealous. Rachel was much younger than I and you might say her future husband just fell into her lap. Jacob was our cousin. He came while we were watering our sheep. He took one look at Rachel and fell madly in love. It is the custom for a man to present a dowry to the family of his future bride. Since Jacob had no money, he offered to work seven years for our father in order to marry Rachel.

At this time, Laban did not tell Jacob of the custom that the older daughter must be married first. Therefore, Jacob worked the seven years as he had promised, and went to claim his bride.

My father was not a truthful person. However, he agreed to the wedding of Jacob and Rachel, and began organizing the wedding feast. He invited everyone in the neighborhood to celebrate. There was much drinking and partying. My father took me aside and told me to put on my sister's wedding dress. He shared his plan with me, and to be honest, it sounded exciting. I knew it was wrong, but a part of me wanted to get even with my sister who had overshadowed me all our lives. In addition, during the seven years Jacob had worked for my father, I had fallen in love with him. I did not intend to be deceitful; I just went along with my father's plan.

Leah, you are like so many of us who do not set out to sin; sometimes it just sneaks up on us. In those days, it was the custom to take the bride to the bedchamber of her husband in silence and darkness on the wedding night. This worked well for what Laban had planned. However, it was not according to the agreement Laban had made with Jacob.

I will also have to admit that I had an active part in the deception. I could have told Jacob at any time I was not Rachel. I did not, so the marriage was consummated. Jacob became very angry when he realized he had been tricked. I was his wife now, and it could not be changed. Because of his love for Rachel, he agreed to work seven more years for my father. My father agreed to give Rachel to him after the bridal week was over.

I can just imagine the humiliation of your position. Every bride awaits her wedding night with great anticipation. However, your wedding night ended in complete rejection. You were given away by your father and coerced into playing an active part in the deception. Even though you admitted you were somewhat pleased with the plan, I am sure it was not easy being married to a man whose heart belonged to your sister. We cannot help feeling a little sorry for Rachel. She must have suffered great distress at seeing her sister married to the man who was to be her husband.

The deed was done, and I longed to be a good wife to Jacob. However, I had much to endure the next few years. I asked Yahweh many times for forgiveness for my part in the deception.

Again, do not be too hard on yourself. We know you must have felt the indignity of the situation, always conscious of not being your husband's first choice. We know God comforts the afflicted in special ways as He did you. Scripture tells us the Lord saw you were unloved and opened your womb. You were blessed with many sons.

My sons made life worth living for me. I named my first son Reuben, which means, "Behold a son." I was hoping my husband would love me now, but it did not happen. He still treated me as someone to bear children. I named my second son Simeon, which means "One who hears." I had now borne Jacob two sons, but his heart was still hard towards me.

I cannot even imagine what you were going through. The name you gave Simeon, "One who hears," reflects a mournful heart. Your third son was named Levi. It was a desperate attempt to make Jacob bind himself to you in a deeper way. However, you were still as unloved by your husband as before. It is easy to imagine the problems in this home with two sisters married to the same man. Rachel had Jacob's love, but you bore him sons. As we look at the names you gave your sons, we can see your heartbreak.

With the birth of my fourth son, God finally got through to me. He helped me break free from the vicious cycle of rejection and worthlessness by refusing to give in to my circumstances. I chose no longer to be a victim. I took the focus off the immediate circumstances and placed my full attention and confidence in the Lord.

In naming your three previous sons, Leah, you chose names that reflected the suffering and loneliness you felt. However, with the birth of your fourth son, you had risen above this hopelessness. You named this newborn son Judah, in honor of the Lord who had sustained and comforted you throughout your long years of despondency and loneliness. Judah means "Praise," because you had finally learned to praise the Lord. God honored you in your role as the mother of Judah. Judah was an ancestor of Jesus Christ.

I had finally learned that praise in all situations is the vital key to accepting your life as it is. I still desired my husband's love, but now I was content to find favor in the Lord. My sister had become very jealous of me over the years because I gave Jacob sons while she was not able to have children. I heard her once say to Jacob, "Give me children or I die." Her life was not easy either. Eventually, Rachel gave birth to her first child, which she named Joseph. Then, as we were on our way back to Jacob's homeland, my little sister died giving birth to her second son, Benjamin.

What a sad ending for the beautiful Rachel. Rachel and Jacob's story is one of the great love stories of the Bible. When

I reflect on her cry to God, "Give me children or I die," could it be that her too impatient cry was heard and answered? She did have children, but with them, came her death. How little she knew what she had asked. With the death of Rachael, you took your place beside your husband as his chief wife.

After Rachel's death, I realized the life of Rachel, Jacob, and I had all been part of God's master plan. The Lord had promised Jacob his descendants would be as numerous as the dust of the earth. However, instead of waiting for God to work out His plan, he fell in love with Rachel, a woman who would die giving birth to her second son. If Jacob had been permitted to follow his own plans, God's promise would not have been fulfilled, or would have been fulfilled another way. I was not a part of Jacob's plan; however, I was an important component in God's plan. Not bragging, but my third son Levi became the ancestor of Israel's priesthood, including Moses, Aaron, Zacharias, and John the Baptist. My fourth son, Judah, was the ancestor of the house of David, the kingly family that included Joseph, the husband of Mary, the mother of Christ. God is so good!

* * *

Leah's story is one of mystery and intrigue. We do not understand how God can use someone's deception as an instrument to accomplish His purposes. However, God was at work in every circumstance in the life of Leah, just as He is always at work in the circumstances of our lives. We saw how He protected Leah, and how He finally fulfilled His promise to Jacob. Just as God had used Jacob's deception of Isaac, as a means to accomplish his own will, He used Laban's deception of Jacob for the same purpose. When will we learn God is in control?

THOUGHTS FOR DISCUSSION
FROM THE LIFE OF LEAH

- Leah and her sister were defined by their looks. Do you think women today are still being defined by their looks? How would you define yourself?

- Leah was hated, despised, rejected, and just tolerated because of her ability to produce children. Have you ever struggled with low self-esteem or some of the same problems Leah experienced? How did you overcome them?

- Leah resisted the urge to whine about her situation. God was aware of her situation. He favored her by continuing to allow her to give her husband sons when her sister was unable to have a child. Do you accept your lot in life and wait for God to take care of the circumstances?

- What evidence do you see in Leah's life that proves she eventually matured in her relationship with Yahweh? Have you ever come to a place in your spiritual life when you discovered some life-giving truth? Were you like Leah who had to come to the point of desperation before she came to a place of praise? Tell of your experience.

- Look in First Corinthians 1:27-29 and see if the truth we find there fits our unloved Leah. How has Leah been "foolish?" In what way is Leah viewed as weak? How might the word lowly suit Leah?" What things might Leah "not possess?" How might God use all of the above for His glory?

- Scripture tells us "All things work together for good for those who love the Lord." How do you explain this in Leah's story?

AN INNOVATIVE MOTHER
(JOCHEBED)
EXODUS 2:1–10

You may never have heard the name of our visitor for today. Her name is only specifically mentioned twice in Scriptures; however, her children are well known. Her oldest son, Aaron, grew up to be a High Priest. Her daughter, Miriam, a prophetess, served alongside her brothers on the long journey to the Promised Land. Moses was chosen by God to lead the Israelites out of Egyptian bondage. I understand the world was not a very safe place, especially when your youngest son was born.

Our lives were hard. The Pharaoh became afraid the Israelites were becoming too numerous, so he issued an edict that mid-wives should kill all Hebrew male children at birth. When my youngest son was born, I realized God had destined him for some special purpose. This premonition was something that only a mother could understand. I knew I could not let my baby die, so I hid him in the donkey stable and food storage room. When he was three months old, I knew I could no longer hide him.

I cannot even imagine what it would be like to have your child under a death sentence. However, you served a God who had been faithful in the past, and you trusted Him to be faithful again. You were able to develop a plan that was a little risky, but it was a time for drastic measures. Jochebed, you are a woman of great faith. Tell us about your plan.

In praying to God to give me wisdom, He brought to mind something I had observed many times. Every day at about the same time and place, Pharaoh's daughter and her maidens came to bathe in the Nile River. Miriam and I worked day and night weaving a little basket from the long stems of the papyrus plant. I chose that particular plant for I knew it would be a protection against crocodiles. We plastered the inside of the little basket with clay so it would be smooth and watertight. We used asphalt as a sealant. When it was finished, I held my baby close one last time, prayed for his safety, and placed him in the basket. Miriam and I hid the basket in the reeds near the edge of the river.

It must have taken a great deal of faith to leave your baby there in the Nile River! You had called on God to protect him, and you had faith He would answer your prayers. You placed the basket among the tall reeds for protection from the weather. Miriam stayed nearby while you hid in the bushes. I am sure it must have seemed like an eternity as you waited for Pharaoh's daughter and her entourage to appear.

All sorts of thoughts went through my mind. I wondered if she would come today, if she would notice how beautiful he was, or if she would have him killed instantly. However, even as these thoughts ran through my mind, I heard my Savior say, "Just trust me!" I had trusted him enough to develop this plan, now I must be patient while He worked it out according to His will. Finally, I saw her coming. As she neared the little basket, my baby began to cry. The princess ordered one of her maidens to bring the basket to her. My prayers were answered. My baby's helpless cries touched her heart.

This was the moment Miriam stepped forward and offered to get one of the Hebrew women to nurse the baby. The princess agreed, and Miriam ran to where you were hiding in the bushes. Your plan worked, and you were reunited with your son.

I thanked God every day I was able to watch over my son until he was seven years of age. I praised God that my child, as the adopted son of the princess, would receive the best education available in a king's palace. He would be raised as a privileged son of the princess. I praised God as I watched over him as he romped and played each day in Pharaoh's palace. I was able to rock him to sleep each night. I was able to teach him the sacred traditions of Israel and of God's divine promise to Abraham and his descendants. I wanted him to know the history of his heritage.

Jochebed, I am sure the character of Moses was developed as he listened to you share your belief in God. You taught him what it meant to be a Hebrew, one of God's chosen people. God used your courageous act of saving and hiding your baby to begin His plan to rescue His people from Egypt. The whole character of Moses displays your holy guidance. However, as he grew up, you had to give him back to the Princess. That must have hurt a great deal.

It did hurt greatly to turn him over to Pharaoh's daughter. I was thankful for the years I had raising him; however, I did wonder if God spared him from death only to have him become a pagan Egyptian living the life of a prince. Even though my arms ached, I had promised to follow God wherever He led. All I could do now was pray for my son.

You had taught Moses from an early age what it meant to be a member of the Hebrew race. As he grew older, he noticed the plight of the Hebrew slaves. Jochebed, will you tell us about an incident that made him leave the Egyptian palace permanently.

Many years later Moses came to visit his people, and observed the cruel way we were treated as slaves. When he saw an Egyptian beating one of his brethren, he killed the Egyptian and buried his body in the sand. The Pharaoh called for his death, and Moses fled to the desert. It was in the desert that Moses encountered God. It was at the burning bush he met God in person and received the commission that framed his life. I never saw my son again; however, God comforted me with the knowledge that I had prepared him for just such a mission.

* * *

We are sure Moses remembered the teachings of his mother throughout his life. Jochebed may not have understood why she had to go through so much pain in raising Moses; but she did know God was in charge of their lives. That knowledge gave her the courage to do what she had to do in order to see that her son lived. Moses evidently did not have an easy life. Leading a group of undisciplined, complaining people would have been very hard. It took patience, humility, and great faith. It was not easy dealing with his own sins, and the sins of his own brother and sister. Even though Moses failed to live up to his calling many times, God used him in a mighty way. Yahweh made a covenant with Moses and the Israelites at Mt. Sinai and Moses spent his life working to shape the Israelites into a nation. Moses has gone down in history as one of the greatest Jewish leaders. We would guess this is due to the early teachings and prayers of a godly mother. Jochebed placed her faith in God and trusted Him with the outcome.

THOUGHTS FOR DISCUSSION
FROM THE LIFE OF JOCHEBED

- What preparation did Jochebed make as she devised a plan to save her baby son? What would have been the dangers of carrying out the plan? What were her fears in placing her baby in the little boat?

- Jochebed probably took every opportunity to teach her young son the Holy Scriptures and instill in him a love for the people of his heritage. How was this part of God's plan for the future of the Israelites?

- Do you take every opportunity to teach your children the scriptures? What is the advantage or disadvantage of teaching them while they are young?

- Eventually Jochebed had to give her young son up to go live in the palace as the son of the pagan princess. How do you think Jochebed reacted? How would you have reacted?

- Do you think Jochebed asked God why it had to happen this way? How do you think God feels when we ask why when something bad happens to us?

- We can be sure she continued to pray for him throughout his life. We give our children up to go out into a sinful world. Are we as diligent in praying for them throughout their lives?

- Jochebed taught Moses to rely on God, and God used him to lead His people out of bondage. At what point in Moses' life do you think Jochebed finally understood the pain of letting him go?

- When God asks us to follow when we don't understand why or how, do we realize that He has a plan for our lives? How hard is it to let go of our plans and dreams and just leave it in God's hands to work out the details? Give examples in your life

SING UNTO THE LORD (MIRIAM)
EXODUS 2:1–10;
NUMBERS 12:1–16

Our guest today is probably best known as the sister of Moses. Even at a young age, Miriam's courage and decisive actions saved the life of her little brother and was instrumental in allowing him to be raised by their mother.

Miriam, you probably grew up feeling very protective toward Moses. Can you tell us what happened to Moses when the Egyptian princess found him?

Even though Moses was just a baby when he went to live in the palace, we were thrilled that he would receive the best education available. Our one fear was that he would also be exposed to idolatry. During the seven years, our mother was able to care for him, she taught him Hebrew heritage, and to respect the one true God. Things went well until Moses was grown. Once during a visit with his Hebrew friends, he saw an Egyptian beating one of the Hebrew slaves. Moses killed the Egyptian and hid his body in the sand. When Pharaoh heard about the slaying, he gave orders to have Moses killed. Moses had to flee to the Midian desert.

That is quite a story within itself, but it was only the beginning. It was here that God spoke to Moses from the burning bush, and told him he would lead the Israelites out of Egypt. I can imagine Moses saying, "Why me. Lord?

You know I don't speak so good." He made other excuses because he felt inadequate for the job God was asking him to do. The next part of Moses' story involves you and your other brother, Aaron. God would not accept Moses' excuse. He told Moses that Aaron would speak for him.

Yes, it was while Moses was in the desert, God spoke to him, and called him to lead His people out of bondage and into the Promised Land. It was during this time Moses asked Aaron and me to join him for the monumental task God had asked him to do for His people. We went through many different plagues and trials as God dealt with the Pharaoh. However, finally we were ready to go to the Promised Land.

What a thrilling, exciting time. The Egyptians were glad to see you go because they knew the plagues were God's judgment on them, so they gave you money and jewels to help you on your long journey. The trip was long and hard, and it was during this time that you became known as a prophetess and you led alongside Moses and Aaron. Miriam, exactly what does a prophetess do?

As a prophetess, I worked to encourage people to obey God. I had a ministry to the women, because you know how a bunch of women can gripe, especially on such a long journey we were undertaking. We had many trials along the way; however, God supplied our every need, providing a cloud by day and fire by night to lead us. God also provided manna so we never wanted for food. Water was scarce, but when we listened to the Lord, we had plenty. Moses depended on me to advise him, and asked my opinion often.

What an amazing display of God's protection. Scripture tells us the Egyptians had second thoughts about letting their slave labor leave. **Pharaoh and his army pursued you, but again God protected you. Tell us what happened when you came to the Red Sea.**

With the Egyptian army in hot pursuit, it seemed impossible that we could cross the Red Sea. However, as Moses stretched out his hand over the sea, we were able to walk across on dry land. We looked from where we came and saw the Egyptian army following in hot pursuit. Once again, as He always is, God was in control. As soon as the last Hebrew set foot on the other side, the waters rushed over the Egyptian army, and not a single person survived.

We know that with everyone safe, it was time to praise the Lord for His watchful care. Music had always played an important part in Israel's worship and celebration, so all the Israelites expressed their love and thanks to God by singing and dancing before Him. Moses composed a Song of Deliverance that lifted the heart and voices of the people outward and upward. After having been delivered from great danger, I can imagine the songs of praise being lifted to the Lord. Miriam, I assume you were one of the leaders.

Yes, I grabbed my tambourine, and led all the women in rhythm and dance. At that moment, we realized what God had done for us. Our only thought was to praise Him for His protection and love. I could praise Him and lead others to praise Him through my music. God gave me that talent and I wanted to use it to glorify Him. We had much to be thankful for at this moment.

That must have been a mountaintop experience. However, I think you found, as we all do at some time or another, you could not rest on those experiences. Satan's plan of

attack is always to come with a vengeance after a truly spiritual experience. That happened to you, didn't it, Miriam?

I am sorry to say it did. I am not proud of what I did, but I want to share it because maybe it will help someone else. I am ashamed to admit that sometime after the incident of the Red Sea, Aaron and I came to be a little jealous of all the attention God was bestowing on Moses. After all, God had called the three of us to be leaders, but Moses was getting all the recognition. In addition, after Moses' first wife Zipporah passed away, he married an Egyptian, a Cushite woman. I felt he should have married a Hebrew or better yet, stayed single. I could not stand the thought of an Ethiopian raised above myself, a proud daughter of Israel. I was no longer the most important woman in his life. As his popularity grew my bitterness and jealously grew.

Sometimes people argue over minor disagreements leaving the real issue untouched. The real issue of your complaint was your growing jealousy of Moses' position and influence. Since you could not find fault with the way Moses was leading the people, you chose to criticize his wife. God was furious with you, and "took you to the woodshed," didn't He?

We certainly trembled as God reminded us that He was in charge. He had chosen Moses and had spoken with him face to face. I never want to see my God furious with me again. Aaron begged God not to punish us for our sin. God didn't reply to Aaron; however, when I looked down at my hands, they were white as snow—I had leprosy. Even though I had held a grudge against him, Moses acted toward me in a spirit of love. He cried out to the Lord to heal me. When he saw me leprous, Moses may have remembered he once had been stricken with leprosy. Through his own experience, Moses had learned our God could cause or cure any kind of problem. God heeded the cry of Moses on my behalf, and said I should be banished from the camp, but after seven days, I could return. I deserved so much more punishment. When I returned to camp, I was a different person. Even though God had forgiven me, I had to make restitution with my brother, which I did as quickly as I could. It was just a reminder to me that God forgives sin but does not always take away the consequences.

Miriam, yours is an incredible story. The lesson you learned is an important one, and one we should all learn. I am sure your heart was touched by your brother's love. Though you were shut out of camp for seven days, you were not shut out of the hearts of those you led so courageously. Though wearied from their long wanderings and impatient at every delay in reaching the Promised Land, Scripture tells us the people did not continue on their journey until you were able to join them. The people you had led so courageously on the journey this far stood by you and waited until you were well again. Together you all marched on toward the Promised Land. The three of you were again leading the way praising God for the newborn Israel.

THOUGHTS FOR DISCUSSION
FROM THE LIFE OF MIRIAM

- Miriam loved her little brother and helped her mother save his life when he was a baby. However, when Moses married, she became critical of his choice of a wife. Why would Miriam be critical of the woman Moses married?

- What are some reasons that we justify offering "constructive criticism"?

- Jealousy can be a problem in each of our lives. Is there jealousy in the church? Give some examples. Can you offer solutions on how to overcome jealousy?

- If you were in this story, which person would you want as a friend? Which person would you want to avoid? Give reasons.

- Tell how the characteristics and actions of the people in the story are still present in our world today.

- Search your heart. What similarities in this story do you see in your life?

- Even though Miriam had been a leader of the Israelite women, God would not allow her to enter the Promised Land. Do you think it was unfair punishment? Give reasons why or why not.

- Has God ever worked in your life when you knew without a doubt that it was punishment for some sin? What was your first plan of action?

- What lesson have you learned from Miriam's life?

FAITH AS STRONG AS A
SCARLET CORD (RAHAB)
JOSHUA 2:1–24; 6:1–27

We are privileged today to have as our guest a woman who (how shall I say this) was a practitioner of the "oldest profession" and ran a house of ill repute.

What she is trying to say is that I was a prostitute. I ran a whorehouse, and decent people did not want to associate with me. In my day, there were two kinds of prostitutes. There were religious ones who worked at the Canaanite temple, and the run-of-the-mill harlots who worked for cash. I was the second kind. I don't mind saying that because, even though I am not proud of my past, it gives me opportunity to tell you what an awesome God we serve.

Rahab, I am so glad that God included your story in the Bible. Stories about the God of the Israelites had been circulating for some time. Therefore, we can understand your fear when you heard the Israelites were on their way to attack your home town of Jericho. Your home was built next to the wall that surrounded the city of Jericho. You were in a very vulnerable position.

Yes I was, and I shared the general mood of fear with the rest of Jericho's population. I knew my home would be a hard one to miss since it was built against the town wall at the gate. I had built the home there to provide a place for weary men to spend the

*night, and partake of "other amenities" I offered. I feared I would
be the first home invaded. While I waited for the attack, two men
appeared at my door. I knew instantly they were different. They
were not interested in the amenities I offered. They explained they
were on a mission to check out Jericho, and see how they could
capture it. My house with the high roof was a perfect place to spy.
They had been seen coming into my house, and I knew eventually
the men of Jericho would come looking for them.*

**God was obviously already speaking to your heart
because you hid the two men. When the king's men came,
they ordered you to bring out the two men that were seen
coming into your home. Rahab, you were faced with a very
difficult choice. You knew your decision now would deter-
mine whether you lived or died.**

*God had been dealing with my heart. Just hearing all the
awesome ways God had worked in the lives of the Israelites, I
knew God had to be with them. I could not let my past define my
future. I believed the arrival of these two men on my doorstep
was divinely ordained from God. I felt it was a sign that my
family and I would be saved by trusting in these two men, and
in the God they served.*

**It seems the God of Heaven is not an ordinary God! He is
all-powerful! How did you respond to the King's men?**

*I hate to admit it, but I lied. However, I knew God knew my
heart and would forgive me. I admitted the two men had been
there but said I did not know where they were from, or where they
went. The king's men believed me, and went looking for the spies.*

**It was then you went to the rooftop and spoke with the
spies. You told them you knew how God had parted the Red**

Sea, and how their God had defeated all their enemies along the way. You asked for a promise from them. Wasn't that being a little bold, seeing that they were spies about to take over your city?

Maybe it was, but since I had just risked my life to save them, I felt it was the least they could do for me. They were gracious and kind. The men assured me if I would continue to protect them; they would keep their promise when Jericho was destroyed. I think my newfound faith in God allowed me to trust these two strangers to keep their word.

Faith flowed in both directions, didn't it? These men had the faith to trust you because of your newfound faith in God, and you were able to have faith in their promise because you could see they were godly men. This was really a God-size miracle. Tell us how you got the two men over the wall.

I will tell you a secret. Over the years I had learned how to help men escape from my house. There had been husbands escaping jealous wives and politicians escaping angry citizens. Many times, I had let a man down on a strong rope. I used this means of escape again for my new God-given friends. Only this time, I used a scarlet rope so the Israelites would know the house to be saved. I let the men down the side of the wall, and told them to hide for at least three days until the king's men gave up searching for them.

Rahab, you used a scarlet cord so the Israelites would recognize your house and spare you and your family. I think it means more than that. The color scarlet reminds us of *The Scarlet Letter*, of hussies in red dresses and the red light district. Remember, Scripture says, "Though your sins are like scarlet, they shall be as white as snow." Were you thinking about this when you chose a scarlet cord?

Yes, the scarlet cord was a wonderful reminder that God had taken away my sins. As I threw the scarlet cord out that window, it was symbolic to me that I was throwing out the old life and putting on the new. Because of the grace of God, I could appear clean before my God because He has thrown out all my scarlet sins much as I threw out the scarlet cord.

Scripture tells us that when the Israelites came, Jericho was tightly shut up to protect the residents. No one went out, and no one came in. I can imagine the tension going on in your house, which now was filled with extended family. For seven long days and nights, the Israelites marched around your city. How did you handle that?

It was nerve-wracking. It was so quiet out there with just the sound of soldiers marching around the city. This went on day after day until we wanted to scream, "Just do something; let the battle begin!" However, they just kept walking around the city doing and saying nothing.

On the seventh day, the walk began as usual, but something different happened. The seventh time around, the priests sounded the trumpet blast, the army gave a loud shout, and the walls of the city came tumbling down. God had given them the city! Joshua gave orders that only those in the house with the scarlet cord were to be spared. I am sure as you waited you were holding your breath to see if the men would keep their promise. What happened next?

The Israelites charged in, took the city and dedicated it to the Lord. I had a few fearful moments wondering if we would be saved; however, the spies came in and led us to safety. When

I left that city, I left my old life behind and began a new life with God.

That is a wonderful story of how God takes care of His people. Rahab, I understand a little romance happened here in the midst of all the destruction. Tradition has it that one of the unnamed spies was a man called Salmon. He saw you embrace his God with passionate abandon, and he fell in love.

Whether or not he was one of those spies I cannot say; after all, he was a spy. However, I will say that God did bless, and I did end up marrying a man named Salmon. God is so good. I learned that by trusting God, your past does not have to define your future. I am a living example of that. God blesses when you are in His will. He saved my extended family and me, and gave me a wonderful new family.

* * *

So there you have it—Rahab's story in her own words. However, wait; there is more to this story. In Matthew 1:5–6, we read that Salmon was the father of Boaz, whose mother was Rahab; Boaz was the father of Obed, whose mother was Ruth. Obed was the father of Jesse, and Jesse was the father of King David. The ex-harlot Rahab was in the royal line of David, and the ancestry of our Lord and Savior Jesus Christ. Isn't it wonderful that God can use anyone who is completely dedicated to Him? That gives me hope.

THOUGHTS FOR DISCUSSION
FROM THE LIFE OF RAHAB

- God often works through people like Rahab, whom we are inclined to reject. Rahab was defined by her past. Have you ever felt defined by your past?

- Have you broken free from your past? If so, share how you did so. If not, what is keeping you from doing so?

- What evidence do you see that the Holy Spirit had already been speaking to Rahab's heart before the spies came to her home?

- Rahab was deceptive and disobedient to the laws of her country; do you think God ordained her actions? Why or why not?

- What do you think was the significance of the scarlet cord to Rahab?

- What is the significance of the scarlet cord to us?

- How did God reward Rahab?

- Why do you think God destroyed Jericho, and why was Rahab the only one who was saved?

- What lesson did you learn from Rahab?

HERE COMES THE
JUDGE (DEBORAH)
JUDGES 4:4–24; 5:1-31

Before I introduce our visitor for today, let me give you the background for her story. After the death of Joshua, the Israelites began a series of cycles of sinning, worshiping idols, being punished, and crying out for help. God would rescue them by sending a judge to bring them back to Him. It was such a time as this our visitor for today became known. Deborah was the fourth and only female judge of Israel. Her moral authority was regarded as appointed by the Lord, and her judgment was greatly sought and highly trusted. We are fortunate she is with us today. Deborah, tell us how you came to be a judge.

I did not set out to be a judge. I was happy taking care of my home and husband. For twenty years, Jabin, king of Canaan, had oppressed my people. They destroyed our vineyards, dishonored our women, and killed our children. I began meeting with the townspeople under the olive trees near our home. They had become discouraged and had given up hope. My heart went out to them as I tried to remind them they must stay faithful to God. I felt the men of Israel had faltered in their leadership of my people, so God led me to rise up and denounce this fear and complacency. I carried in my heart the great hope that God would come to deliver us if we would honor Him.

We can see why you became popular with the people. Your religious zeal and patriotic fervor must have somehow awakened in them the enthusiasm for immediate action against the enemy. Who better to lead them than you, who had awakened in them a renewed dedication to God? You went from being a counselor to being a judge. Judges in those days had more duties than judges do today. They were chieftains, warriors, and God's representatives. God was looking for someone to lead His people. He must have recognized in you the humble spirit and leadership He was seeking.

It was not easy being a woman; however, I had God on my side. He gave me the courage to summon Barak, one of Israel's most capable military men, to help me develop a plan of action against the enemy. Barak expressed fear of the large army of Jabin. He was afraid of Sisea, the commander of their 900 chariots of iron. Barak thought they were too strong for the feeble army of Israel. I reminded him God had led us out of Canaan, and had given up victory over Pharaoh and his great army. I had to make him realize God was mightier than the enemy's army. Barak was not convinced at first. I think he may have been a little reluctant to take orders from a woman.

I am sure Barak sensed the spiritual insight you possessed, and feeling the urgent need for your presence, he stated he would not go to battle unless you went with him. That demonstrated the general's great confidence in God's leadership and guidance in your life. Did you go to battle with him?

I was glad to go with him; however, I did tell him if I went with him, the Lord would give Sisera into the hands of a woman. God had assured me He would be with us. Although we were not armed as well as the Canaanite army, we went forward armed with our faith in God. As our small army was about to meet the large army of the Canaanites, God took over. A great storm of sleet and hail burst over the plains from the east into the face of Sisera's men. Their army was defeated by the beating rain and biting cold.

Wow, that would make a good movie! As you watched the storm lash your enemy, I am sure your army believed even more in God's providential care. I understand the rain was so violent that Sisera's heavy iron chariots sank deep in the mud and your army was able to capture them easily. Sisera escaped and ran for his life through the blinding rain. He escaped from the battle, but God was not finished with him. Sisera abandoned his chariot and stumbled through the rain to the tent of Jael. Tell us about Jael.

Jael was the wife of one of Sisera's men and he felt safe going to her tent. Jael welcomed him, and gave him warm milk and lodging. Thinking he was safe, Sisera soon fell sound asleep. While he slept, Jael took a peg used to stretch the tents on the ground, and with a hammer drove it into Sisera's temple. While her husband was loyal to Sisera's forces, Jael felt no loyalty.

Barak was in hot pursuit of Sisera, and soon came to the tent of Jael and found Sisera dead. Deborah, I am sure your words must have come to Barak's mind: "For the Lord shall sell Sisera into the hand of a woman."

Barak was not too happy about a woman being the one to kill Sisera, but he had to accept it. However, I think he did have a new respect for women. Barak and I were so grateful for the victory God had given us, we composed the Song of Deborah. We were careful to give God all the credit for defeating the Canaanite army. From the day the Israelites saw God subdue the Canaanite king, Israel became strong against King Jabin, until they finally destroyed him. We never failed to praise God for His goodness and mercy to us.

How appropriate the two of you would sing praises to God for such an outstanding victory. Deborah, your life challenges us to be available when God calls, and to have faith and rely on Him. Your life demonstrates what a person can accomplish when God is in control and wise leaders choose good helpers.

THOUGHTS FOR DISCUSSION
FROM THE LIFE OF DEBORAH

- Would you have chosen a woman to lead into military battle? Why or why not? God chooses wise leaders by His standards—not ours. Would you be willing to go into battle if God leads?

- Deborah is admired because she did not deny or resist her position in the culture as a woman and wife, but she never allowed herself to be hindered by it either. What was the first priority in Deborah's life? What is the first priority in your life?

- What does scripture tell us Deborah and Barak were armed with when they went into battle?

- Deborah's story reminds us that we need to be available when God calls. If you sense what you think is a call from God, what should be your first action?

- God was Deborah's source of justice in dealing with others. Examine your relationships. How hard is it to always deal justly with your spouse, children, coworkers, and friends who have hurt you? What is your plan of action?

- Are we always careful to give God all the praise and honor due Him for the victories He accomplishes through us, or do we claim some of the glory or praise for ourselves?

• Deborah's legacy was one of justice for all people and motivating others to follow God's direction. What legacy would you like to leave?

• How is Deborah's story relevant to women today?

GOD'S DEALINGS WITH
A WAYWARD CHILD
(SAMSON'S MOTHER)
JUDGES 13, 14, 15, 16:1-31

You may not know our guest today, so let me introduce you to her. This is Mrs. Manoah, the mother of Samson. The Manoah family lived at a time when the Lord had delivered the Israelites into the hands of the Philistines for 40 years because of their rebellion. Times were sad and hard. Mrs. Manoah had been unable to have a child, so you can imagine her happiness when the angel of the Lord appeared to her and announced she would soon become pregnant and have a child. Mrs. Manoah, did the angel tell you how to raise your child?

He just told me I would have a son and he was to be dedicated to God as a Nazirite. A Nazirite was a person who took a vow to be set apart for God's service. The angel told us that he could never cut his hair, touch a dead body, or drink anything containing alcohol. He said our son was chosen by God to rescue Israel from the Philistines. We knew he was a special child, and I am afraid that instead of asking God for guidance on how to raise him, we spoiled him. We had waited so long for a child, and now here was this strong, perfect child. We were so proud of him. Can you blame us for spoiling him?

We can certainly understand your spoiling him, because many of us have done the same thing. Samson was born to do a great work for God – to rescue Israel from the Philistines. To help accomplish God's plan, he was given enormous physical strength. What happened, Mrs. Manoah?

We tried to raise him in the Lord. We did the best we could. Looking back, I realize we could have done more. We could have taught him scriptures, and gone with him to the synagogue regularly. I am afraid we were not very consistent in our discipline. Samson wasted his strength on practical jokes and getting out of scrapes.

Do not beat yourself up Mrs. Manoah; that happens to many people. You just do the best you can at the time, and leave the rest up to the Lord. I think many parents have regrets in that area. Samson was used to getting his own way, and when he saw a beautiful Philistine woman he wanted, he ordered your husband to get her for him. Samson must have known from Old Testament scriptures that God was very clear about his prohibition of intermarriage between the Israelites and the surrounding pagan nations.

We tried to talk to him, but he would not listen. To make matters worse, we knew he did not really care for this girl as a person. He just saw her and wanted her. We knew it was wrong for him to marry a pagan Philistine when there were a number of good Jewish girls that would have loved to marry him. We were afraid he was asking for heartache by rebelling against Jehovah and us. He was going against everything his Nazirite vows stood for. It broke my heart, but there was nothing we could do. He was an adult now, and responsible for his own choices.

Samson could overcome lions and Philistines, but he could not overcome his own lust for beautiful women. How sad. I understand on his way to get the girl he encountered a lion. The lion charged him, and he tore it apart limb by limb. Sometime later, some honeybees had built a nest in the lion's body. Samson loved practical jokes and getting out of scrapes, so he devised a riddle about the honeycomb. The girl cried and begged until Samson gave her answer to the riddle. She gave the answer to the men in the town, and the Philistines came to capture him

Yes, I'm sorry to say when they came to capture him, the Spirit of the Lord came upon Samson, and he killed 30 men of that town. He went back for his wife and found her father had given her to his best friend at the wedding. Samson was so angry he caught 300 foxes, took torches, and turned them tail to tail. He put a torch between each pair of tails, and set fire to the torches. He turned the foxes loose into the standing grain of the Philistines, and it burned their grain and olive orchards. Oh, how our hearts ached. We knew God had no part in this. It was Samson venting his personal resentment and anger. The anger of the Philistines increased against him.

There were other incidents in Samson's life, and God miraculously delivered him each time. After defeating the Philistines, Samson was appointed Israel's Judge. For 20 years, he carried out those duties without incident. If the story had just ended there, it would have been a story of triumph. Samson had learned at this point that God was adequate to meet all his needs. However, it did not stop there did it?

We thought he had learned his lesson. However, we have learned that Satan never gives up even as we grow older. Soon

after, Samson became infatuated with a woman named Deli-
lah. Delilah was beautiful, seductive, and straight from the pit
of hell. How could he not see; how could he get involved with
another pagan woman? Meeting this woman was the begin-
ning of his downfall and eventual death. As judge, Samson
had been taking great vengeance on the Philistines, and now
they wanted to capture him. The greedy Delilah was a willing
partner in their plan.

Delilah may have been attracted to Samson, but she cer-
tainly was not in love with him. When the Philistine rulers
offered her 5,500 pieces of silver to collaborate with them in
a scheme to uncover the secret of Samson's great strength,
she readily agreed. She was sure it would be an easy task
since she knew how to handle men.

Delilah kept nagging Samson for the secret of his strength.
Three different times he allowed himself to be bound by the Phil-
istines, and all three times, he broke the ropes easily. It should
have ended there. He should have seen Delilah for what she
was. She was a deceitful woman with honey on her lips and
poison in her heart. She was cold and calculating. How could
my boy be so foolish? Finally, blinded by her beauty and decep-
tive words and actions, Samson gave in to her nagging and
revealed that his long hair was the real secret of his strength.
Then with his head in her lap, she lulled him to sleep and
called for the Philistines to shave off his hair. Samson thought
he would break their bonds as he had in the past, but this time
his strength was gone. He was too weak to resist, so the Philis-
tines captured him.

At that moment, he had given up the last of the condi-
tions of his Nazirite vow, and his relationship with the Lord

was broken. Rather than killing Samson, the Philistines preferred to humiliate him. They gouged out his eyes and subjected him to hard labor in a Gaza prison. As he slaved at grinding grain, his hair began to grow. In spite of his horrible failures and sins of the past, Samson's heart now turned to the Lord and he was humbled. He prayed to God and God answered. Tell us what happened next, Mrs. Manoah.

You cannot imagine how my heart ached seeing my son like this, but I was thankful he had finally humbled himself and turned to the Lord. At a pagan sacrificial ritual, the Philistines paraded their prized prisoner into the temple to entertain the jeering crowds as they worshiped their god of Dagon. It hurt to watch his humiliation. As we watched, we asked God's forgiveness for not disciplining our son as we should have and for not teaching him to have more respect for the vows God had bestowed upon him at birth. God assured us He was in control.

* * *

We know the rest of the story. The house was full of men and women; all the lords of the Philistines were there. On the roof there were 3,000 men and women who looked on and made fun of Samson. Probably during the months of grinding at the mill, Samson thought about his life and came to the realization his strength had been in the Lord. He asked God to strengthen him once again. He grasped the two pillars upon which the house rested, and with all his strength, pulled the roof down killing all the Philistines. God had taken His hand off Samson and allowed him to go his own way. However, when Samson called out to God with a repentant heart, God was there waiting. This is true in our own lives.

THOUGHTS FOR DISCUSSION FROM THE LIFE OF MRS. MANOAH

- What do you see in the life of Samson that makes you think he was an undisciplined child?

- Samson had taken the Nazirite vow of dedication to the Lord. How serious is it to ignore a direct calling of God on your life?

- What bearing do you think Samson's choice of friends had on his failure to live for the Lord? Are you careful about the friends you or your children chose?

- Samson broke every vow he made as a Nazirite. How can loss of faith turn into a form of bondage? What was the bondage in Samson's life?

- Can you give an example of parents who raise their children in the Lord, but the children were rebellious? Were you a rebellious child? When and how did you find your way back?

- How is it possible for God to use a person of faith in spite of his/her sin?

FAITHFULNESS AND LOVE IN ACTION (RUTH AND NAOMI)
BOOK OF RUTH

What a privilege it is to have these two Godly women with us today. Their story took place when the judges ruled in Israel. The story of Ruth and Naomi is woven together so closely that they are almost inseparable. We know more about their relationship than we do about them as individuals. Their story is somewhat unusual because Naomi is an Israelite, and Ruth was born into a Moabite family. Moab was the land east of the Dead Sea and one of the nations that oppressed Israel during the time of the Judges. Naomi, you came from a well-to-do family in Bethlehem. Why did you move to Moab when you knew that country was Israel's sworn enemy?

There was a famine in Canaan, and it was getting worse. My husband Elimelech determined we should go to Moab where he had heard there was plenty to eat. Therefore, we took our two sons and moved to Moab. It was not easy living in a pagan country.

The famine in Israel must have been quite severe for your husband to take you and your sons to live in Moab. Israel had defeated Moab, but there were still tensions between the two. I am surprised Elimelech would move his family there.

You do what you have to do to feed your family. My two sons had not been well, and I just knew they could not survive a severe famine. The years in Moab were not too bad. At least we had food to eat.

Naomi, we know after several years in Moab, your husband died. However, you were not left completely alone. Your two sons had married Moab women. After about ten years, tragedy struck again, and both your sons died. That must have been a very difficult time for you and your daughters-in-law.

Yes, it was very difficult. There was almost nothing worse than being a widow in our day. I felt there was nothing left for me in Moab. I heard God was blessing His people with good crops again in Canaan, so I decided to go back home.

You were smart to go back home. You knew God's law provided the nearest relative of the dead should care for the widow. Even though you were not aware of any relative still living in Israel, you wanted to go home. Even in your desperate situation, you displayed a selfless attitude. You encouraged your daughters-in-law to stay in Moab with their relatives. They were young, and you felt they could probably marry again. Orpah did decide to go back to her home, but Ruth insisted on going with you.

Ruth, we are so happy you are here with us today. We know that you were born and raised in Moab. Will you tell us why you made the decision to leave Moab and go with Naomi to her homeland?

Thank you for having me today. I made that decision because I had learned to love my mother-in-law. I know some people have problems with their mother-in-law, but Naomi is a special person. Over the years, we had shared deep sorrow.

During these times, our affection for one another grew. I grew up worshipping other gods, but in Naomi, I saw a woman who had absolute faith in the one true God. Her life led me to become a believer in her God. I assured Naomi I wanted to go wherever she went, and I wanted her people and her God to be my people and my God.

God certainly was at the center of your relationship with Naomi. When you arrived in Bethlehem, the townspeople were excited to see Naomi. Because of the hardships she had experienced, Naomi asked them to call her Mara. Mara means bitter, and her life had become bitter and sad. Because you were close to Naomi, you understood her disappointment and anguish in her relationship with God. She said she had gone away full, but the Lord had brought her home empty. Ruth, what did she mean by that?

She had left Judah with a husband and sons, but was coming home with neither. She felt God had dealt her a low blow, and she had come back bitter. I do not want you to think harshly of Naomi. She was not rejecting God by openly expressing her pain and bitterness. I do not think God minds if we express our true feelings if we do not overlook the love, strength, and resources He provides in our time of need. Naomi would never do that. She loved God and taught me to depend on Him completely.

I am sure God knew Naomi's heart just as He knows ours when we are overwhelmed and cry out to Him. Ruth, we know when you returned to Bethlehem, you needed to find work to support you and Naomi. It was harvest time, and harvesters were hired to cut down the stalks and tie them into bundles. Israelite law demanded the corners of the fields were not to be touched, and any grain dropped was left for poor people to pick up. You found a field and went to work picking up the dropped grain. You were not sitting around waiting for a handout.

I was not afraid of hard work. I was thankful for the opportunity to earn our food, even though the task was hard. I did not know at the time, but I found myself in a field that belonged to Boaz, a relative of my father-in-law. Boaz allowed his workers to leave extra grain for me to gather. I was surprised he would be so good to a foreigner like me. However, he said he knew how I had helped Naomi since her husband died, and he had asked God to reward me for my faithfulness.

Naomi, can you tell us what happened next?

My daughter-in-law was a hardworking, beautiful woman. It was not long until everyone in Bethlehem knew this about her. It was not surprising when Boaz noticed her. I thanked God for reminding me that Boaz was one of our closest relatives, one of our family redeemers. With God's help, I developed a plan. I told Ruth to prepare herself, put on her nicest clothes, and wait for Boaz to lie down for the night. She was to uncover his feet and lay there. This was a Jewish custom to let him know she was available. I know this was an unconventional plan, but I felt God's leadership.

Ruth, what happened when you followed Naomi's plan?

About midnight Boaz awoke and found me at his feet. He indicated he cared for me, but there was a problem. There was a relative much closer related than Boaz. The other relative had the first right to buy the land left by Elimelech and marry me. Boaz found that the other relative did not want to redeem the land and marry me. That left Boaz free to marry me.

* * *

That is a beautiful love story. God brought great blessings out of Naomi's tragedy. Boaz and Ruth had a son, which added to Naomi's joy. The women in town loved Naomi and praised God for giving her a kinsman- redeemer, and restoring her joy. This story may seem like just a nice story about a relationship between a mother-in-law and her daughter-in-law. However, Ruth and Naomi's story was part of God's preparations for the births of David and of Jesus, the Promised Messiah.

THOUGHTS FOR DISCUSSION FROM THE LIVES OF RUTH AND NAOMI

- As you look at Ruth's pledge of loyalty and love to Naomi, how is this a great proclamation of faith in God?

- Why was it important for Naomi to know that Ruth was committed to the God of Israel before Ruth returned with her to Bethlehem?

- Friendship such as these women enjoyed does not just happen. Ruth and Naomi probably faced some of the same problems we face as we seek to form a bond of love with in-laws. Have you faced some problems in bonding with your in-laws? How did you resolve the situation?

- In her bitterness, Naomi cried out to the Lord. What assurance do we have that God wants to hear our anguish and disappointments?

- Ruth's faith was in God. Her circumstances were tragic, but God provided for her. Has there been a time in your life when your circumstances seemed hopeless and God provided for you? Have you shared that experience with others?

- What is faith? What does faith demand?

- How is Ruth's faith a blessing to us today?

DEVOTED SERVANT
OF GOD (HANNAH)
1 SAMUEL: 1–28; 2:1-11

The story of Hannah our guest for today is very similar to others in the Bible. Hannah lived with her husband and his second wife in the hill country of Ephraim during the times of the Judges. Elkanah's second wife had children, but Hannah was barren. Welcome Hannah. I see that your name means grace, and after reading the story of your life, I would say it is a good description of you. I am sure it must have taken a great deal of grace and prayer to live in a home with a second wife. Was this a difficult arrangement?

It was difficult at times; however, I accepted the arrangement because that was the custom of the day. I never doubted Elkanah's love for me, even though I had been unable to give him a child.

Some people have compared you to Sarah, one of our previous visitors. Would you agree with that comparison?

I am pleased to be compared to Sarah. I have lived my life wanting to be like Sarah, and praying God would give me the same miracle He gave Sarah. Because I was barren, the law of the day said my husband could divorce me if he chose to do so. Elkanah loved me and remained devoted to me, even though my failure to have a child was a social embarrassment. Like Sarah, I spent many years praying for a child.

It must have been difficult for you living in the same household with the second wife and her children. How did you handle this difficult situation?

I tried to spend as much time as possible with my heavenly Father in prayer. I prayed for patience and understanding. I asked God to keep me from becoming bitter and hateful with Peninnah. It was not always easy. I often tried to help with her children, but she did not want my help. In fact, she taunted me about not being able to give my husband a child.

Many women would have become bitter in your situation. Having to share your husband with another woman who was obviously very "fertile," would have been enough without the taunts that came your way. This would cause any woman to be insecure and become bitter. I am sure the stress took its toll on you, and it is little wonder that you were often reduced to tears and could not eat at times. Hannah, tell us about the trip you and Elkanah made to Shiloh.

Every year our family traveled to Shiloh to worship and sacrifice in the Tabernacle. When Elkanah presented his own sacrifice, he then gave portions of the sacrifice to Peninnah and each of her children. He always gave me a special portion. On this particular trip to the Tabernacle, I was feeling discouraged and inadequate as a wife. I begged God to give me a son, and I promised I would give that son back to Him. My life seemed hopeless. I was unable to bear children, I shared my husband with a woman who ridiculed me, my loving husband could not solve my problems, and even the priest misunderstood me.

As you were praying, Eli the priest was watching you. He could see your weakened condition and your lips moving.

Hearing no sound, he thought you were drunk. He scolded you for coming into the Temple drunk. What happened next?

I quickly assured the priest I was not drunk, I was pouring out my heart to the Lord. I did not want the priest to think I was a wicked woman, so I assured him I had been praying out of great anguish and sorrow for a child. The priest surprised me when he said, "In that case, may the God of Israel grant the request you have asked of Him."

That promise must have given you hope. You had also made a promise to God. God keeps His promises, and He expects us to keep ours. Hannah, your prayers were answered, and you eventually had a son. Did you keep your promise to God to give your son back to Him?

I did keep my promise, even though it broke my heart. I did not realize at the time I made the promise to God how hard it was going to be to give up my son. However, I had made a vow, and I was determined to keep that vow. When my son was weaned, we took him to the Temple and presented him to Eli to serve in the house of the Lord. It was hard to leave my son with Eli since I knew Eli's sons were wicked. However, I had made a promise to God, and I had to fulfill that promise.

I think we have learned from your experience that we need to be careful what we promise in prayer because God may just take us up on it. Although we are not in a position to barter with God, He may still choose to answer a prayer that has an attached promise. Hannah, did you see your son after this?

Even though I gave him to the Lord, I visited him regularly. Each year I made robes for Samuel and Eli. I did not see my son as often as I would have liked; however, I was in prayer for him every day. I thanked God for His answer to my prayer for a son. I not only prayed for Samuel, but I also prayed for Eli. I asked God to give him the wisdom to teach and guide my son to serve the Lord.

* * *

Hannah's prayer of praise is found in 1 Samuel 2. We know that Samuel became the last in the long line of Israel's judges. While some of Israel's judges relied more on their own judgment than God's judgment, Samuel's obedience and dedication to God made him one of the greatest judges in Israel's history. Hannah had taught him well.

THOUGHTS FOR DISCUSSION FROM THE LIFE OF HANNAH

- In what way did Hannah fit the meaning of her name, "grace"?

- Did anyone understand Hannah's desire for a child? What were the attitudes of the people surrounding Hannah, her husband, the second wife, and the overly judgmental priest?

- How do you respond to a woman who is unable to have a child? If you have ever been in that situation, how did people respond to you?

- Have you ever tried to bargain with God? How did it turn out?

- Why would Hannah leave her son with Eli, the priest, who had not raised his own sons to be godly men? What would have been your concerns?

- What words would you use to describe Hannah? Why?

- How do you respond to the statement: "A woman is by no means required to be a wife or a mother to be useful to the Lord?" Tell of a single person or a childless mother you know who serves the Lord faithfully.

HOW TO DEAL WITH A DIFFICULT HUSBAND (ABIGAIL)
1 SAMUEL 25:1-42

Abigail, we are so happy to have you with us today. I understand someone has written your life story, and I am intrigued with the title you have given it—*How to Deal with a Difficult Husband*. Can you tell us about your husband?

Yes, my husband was Nabal, a very wealthy, arrogant man who owned property at Carmel. He had a thousand goats and three thousand sheep. It was an arranged marriage, and I had hopes it would work out, but at times my husband could be a very difficult individual. He was an alcoholic and was not a nice person when drunk. At those times, I mostly just tried to stay out of his way. He was mean-spirited and stingy in his dealings with other people. I just did the best I could.

I admire you for that. Tell us about the time you decided to take matters in your own hands.

It was sheep-shearing time, and David and his men were in the Desert of Mao hiding from King Saul. They were camped near my husband's sheep, and they protected the sheep from marauders. This protection afforded by David and his men was part of the reason for Nabal's wartime prosperity. Yet when David came asking for daily provisions for his men, Nabal became belligerent and insulted the very men who had been protecting him.

I understand it made David angry and rightly so. It was dangerous work, but David and his men graciously and freely provided protection. Nabal should have been appreciative for their protection.

You don't know my husband. He is a very difficult man. One of the servants reported to me that David had made Nabal so angry that David ordered his men to strap on their swords. The servant feared a disaster was hanging over our whole household because of Nabal's treatment of King David and his men.

Abigail, what a dangerous situation you found yourself in. I understand you decided to go to David and try to make peace. Your husband would probably have had you killed if he had known what you planned to do. It was very brave of you to take presents and go to David. Were you afraid?

I was afraid but I had to do something. I have children, parents, and a whole house full of servants to think of. I first thought of pleading with Nabal, but I knew that it would not do any good. He was probably drunk any way. I prayed to my God for protection, gathered up food, and went to talk to David.

You are a very brave woman, Abigail. Tell us what happened when you came to David's camp. Weren't you afraid they might think you and your servants were coming to attack them?

As soon as I saw David, I quickly got off my donkey and bowed down. I fell at his feet and said, "My Lord, let the blame be on me alone. May my Lord pay no attention to that wicked man Nabal. I know Nabal is a wicked and ill-tempered man. Please do not pay any attention to him. He is a fool, just as his name suggests. But as for me, your servant, I did not see the men my master sent." I asked David's forgiveness, and said I would pray the Lord would keep him safe.

You were certainly taking your life in your hands. What were you thinking, taking the blame for your spiteful husband? Abigail, you are a beautiful woman, did you ever think of offering yourself to David? That is what most beautiful women probably would have done.

I will have to admit that Satan tempted me just a little by saying, "Why risk your life for Nabal when you could entice David?" I thought of all Nabal's evil ways, and it was tempting to let David kill him. However, I could not do that. I had to trust God with the outcome.

I admire you, Abigail, because it must have been tempting for you to cry out, "It isn't fair. I could not help what my husband did. I don't deserve this." God certainly protected you when David responded favorably to you. Being a typical woman, you even dared to offer him some advice, didn't you?"

I could not help reminding him of God's love for him and God's plan for his life as king of Israel. I told him that he did not need to avenge himself or even protect himself, for he was in God's care and under God's protection.

I understand David's anger disappeared. I would guess your beauty, wisdom, and yes, even your counsel and concern, caused his anger to disappear. You probably won his heart right then. I can imagine he was tempted to pick you up and take you with him, but your commitment to your husband caused him not to do that. He probably went away thinking

Nabal was a fool. What happened when you returned home to Nabal?

I had determined to tell him what I had done whatever the consequences. However, when I returned home he was holding a banquet. He was very drunk, so I told him nothing. The next morning when I told him everything, his heart failed him, and he became like stone. About ten days later he died. I nursed him to the end. I did everything I could do to help him, so I have no guilt. God had intervened and I was free.

What an amazing story. I hope they make a movie of your experiences. I hear that you have a new life now. Would you like to share with us what has happened to you since the time of our story?

Yes, I would love to share with you. When David heard that my husband had passed away, he sent word to me asking me to become his wife. Of course, I said yes. I was ready for the new life God had given me.

* * *

The moral of Abigail's story is not "Do the right thing and God will give you a man who would be king." The moral of her story is "Do the right thing and God will take care of you." God can use your testimony to help all the women who are trying to cope with a difficult husband. We also learn that we should not be afraid to speak out when we have the opportunity.

THOUGHTS FOR DISCUSSION
FROM THE LIFE OF ABIGAIL

- When faced with a difficult, abusive husband, she was loyal and did not give up when the going got tough. Have you ever given up when faced with a tough situation? What were the results?

- Abigail's life shows that life's tough situations can bring out the best in people. Has living with your tough situation brought out the best or worst in you? Explain.

- Like many women today, Abigail found herself in a difficult marriage. Biblical instruction to wives is submission to husbands. What are your feelings about being submissive to an abusive husband?

- Abigail was wise in knowing the right time to explain to her husband about speaking to David. Can you see past the immediate crisis and be patient allowing time for God to get involved in the situation?

- Abigail was not hesitant or afraid to speak to David about God's plan for his future. Are you hesitant or afraid to speak to someone about Christ because their knowledge of scriptures is impressive?

- Abigail had the gift of wisdom. Has there ever been a particular time in your life when you were especially aware that God was giving you wisdom to deal with a difficult situation?

SIN ON A HOT TIN ROOF
(BATHSHEBA)
2 SAMUEL 11:1–26;
1 KINGS 1:11-31

We have a very famous guest with us today. Much has been written about this beautiful woman. On the one hand, she has been envied and admired as part of a very romantic story, but she has also been maligned and blamed for seducing a king. Who is the real Bathsheba? Maybe we will find out today as you share your story with us.

In spite of what you may think about me, I want you to know I am from a God-fearing family, and I was taught right from wrong. I was young and a new bride when my husband, Uriah, went to war. He was one of King David's most trusted generals, and when this story started, he was away fighting the Ammonitish war. I had never been alone until now, and I did not know how to handle my loneliness. This particular evening, I was bored and depressed. It was a hot night, so I went to the rooftop to take my bath. Maybe I wanted someone to see and admire me. My husband had been gone a very long time. Every woman needs to be loved and admired. I am not excusing myself, just telling you what happened.

We know from scripture that this happened at a time when the king had chosen to stay home from the war. Obviously, he was not where he should have been. Were you aware the king had a view of your rooftop from his palace?

Yes, I knew I could be seen from the palace; however, I did not know he was home. His men had gone to war, and if I thought about it at all, I would have assumed he was with them. My only thought was; it was a hot night; I needed a bath, and it would be cooler on the rooftop.

The king had a good view of your house from his palace on the eastern ridge. He had gone to the rooftop for a walk in the cool night air. He could have been feeling sorry that he had stayed home while his men were fighting the war. David had allowed himself to be placed so high on the throne that he found himself all alone. He too, may have been feeling a little lonely. As he walked on the roof, he looked down and saw you bathing. The king was accustomed to wanting and getting. He sent his messengers to find you. What did you think when his messengers came and said the king desired you?

I couldn't help but be a little flattered. What girl wouldn't have been? I knew it was wrong, but I did not think I had the option to refuse the king. I will admit I did not try very hard to refuse. He had sent his messengers to bring me to him, so I went. It was exciting to be chosen by the king.

You went to him, and had sexual relations. I am sure neither of you considered the consequences of your sin in the moment of passion. Bathsheba, what happened after that one night?

He sent me home the next day. A short time later, I found out I was with child, and I panicked. I sent a message to the king, asking him to help me. I wondered how I could ever face my husband with the news I was with child by another man. What do I do now?

Bathsheba, you remind me of young women today caught in sin, and crying out the same thing you cried out. David should have fallen on his face before God and repented. He should have asked for mercy, and begged God to help clean up the mess he had made. However, instead of doing that, he chose to try to solve the problem in his own way. This just increased his sin and guilt, as it always does when we try to cover our sin. He devised a plan of bringing Uriah home from the battlefield. David felt sure Uriah would come home and lay with his wife. As we so often do, David thought he had the perfect solution. However, it did not work that way, did it?

No, it did not work because my husband was a man of integrity. He refused to come home to me out of loyalty to his men on the battlefield. Twice, the king brought Uriah home from the battlefront, and twice he refused to come home to me. When his little schemes did not work, the king gave orders that Uriah be placed in the forefront of the hottest battle. Therefore, my husband died in battle at King David's order. I mourned for my husband, and for the part I had in his death. When the period of mourning was over, David made me one of his wives.

Scripture tells us that the Lord sent Nathan the prophet to David. As a prophet, Nathan was required to confront sin, even the sin of a king. With courage, skill, and tact Nathan made David aware of his sin by telling him the story of two men; one rich, the other poor. The rich man owned many sheep and cattle while the poor man had nothing but a little lamb, which he had raised and loved. One day a guest arrived at the home of the rich man. The rich man took the poor man's lamb, killed it, and served it to his guest. David was furious when he heard the story, and ordered the rich man to die! Then Nathan said to David, "You are that man."

David realized his sin, confessed it to Nathan and to God, and asked forgiveness. Then Nathan told him that while the Lord had forgiven us, our child would die. It was during this time that David wrote Psalm 51, crying out for forgiveness and God's blessing. Many times, I have asked God, Why did my child have to die?

I cannot tell you that, Bathsheba, but I can tell you that the child dying was not a judgment on the child for being conceived out of wedlock. God judges sin and, in reality, you and David both deserved to die; however, God spared your lives and took the child instead. Perhaps the child's death was a greater punishment for you and David than your own deaths would have been. David had risen to the peak of his life and career—when suddenly the devil tripped him up. When he fell on his face before God and asked forgiveness, God forgave him, and restored him to the place he belonged. Will you tell us what your life was like after this?

David's pleas had touched the heart of God. We found that God's heart aches as He disciplines His children. David was still a man after God's own heart. In His mercy and grace, God removed the curse of our sinful union. Through the loss of this child, our union was strengthened as we comforted each other. Eventually, I was able to give David another child. We learned that chastisement is painful, but God never turns His back on us. He disciplines us, and draws us back to a place where He can bless and use us once more.

I want to make it clear again that losing a child is not always the result of sin on the part of the parents. We do not know why some are taken and some are not. David was king of God's holy nation, and had continued to rebel against God in spite of the Holy Spirit's urgings. God could not allow His chosen one to get by with sin. You both had been punished with the death of your son; however, the Lord offered restoration with another son, Solomon, who found favor in His sight.

As King David was nearing death, his fourth son, Adonijah, declared himself king. You knew that unless something was done, you and your son would be killed. Nathan, the prophet came to you with a plan. Will you tell us about that plan?

Nathan advised me to go to the king at once. I was to remind David he had promised my son would be king. Nathan was to come in later and confirm what I had said. I went to the King and did as Nathan suggested. Nathan verified what I had said. I reminded David that if he did not declare Solomon king, we would be killed.

We know that just before he died, David did declare Solomon as king. Bathsheba, we see a mother's heart in your concern and bravery for your son. He was God's choice, as history would prove. It was obvious you were a good mother to Solomon, for he gave you the place of honor as queen mother. It was a place of power and authority.

* * *

I hope that Bathsheba will not be remembered for her early indiscretions, but for her wisdom and leadership as Queen mother. She teaches that God's mercy helps us to embrace our grief, and then release it to live again.

THOUGHTS FOR DISCUSSION
FROM THE LIFE OF BATHSHEBA

- Bathsheba was caught in a chain of events over which she seemingly had no control. Was she responsible for the way she participated in those events? Why or why not?

- Concerning the affair with David, what was Bathsheba's first mistake? What was David's first mistake?

- The consequences of David and Bathsheba's sin reached the second and third generations. Are you aware of some sin your parents passed on to you, and you may be passing on to your children? Explain.

- Read 1 Kings 1:11-14 and answer the following questions:
  a. Why did Nathan go to Bathsheba instead of approaching David himself?
  b. Had David really promised that Solomon would be king?
  c. Was Nathan acting on the Lord's command, or was he trying to ensure that his prophecy would continue to be fulfilled?
  d. Did Bathsheba use manipulation to gain her own way?

- Have you accepted the fact that while we have to live with the natural consequence of sin, God gives us a second chance? Give details of a personal experience.

- There is much controversy concerning whether Bathsheba was a heroine in a romantic novel or if she was a manipulative woman. Give arguments supporting your view.

- Where does Bathsheba fit in the genealogy of Christ?

STAR IN GOD'S PLAN (ESTHER)
BOOK OF ESTHER

We are happy to have Esther visit us today. This story could have come straight out of a best-selling novel. However, yours is a true story. It is a story of God's sovereignty and how He prepared you and Mordecai for the drama that unfolded. Esther, since you are a Jew, how did you happen to be in Persia?

My parents and extended family were taken captive to the Kingdom of Persia following Jerusalem's last stand against Nebuchadnezzar. Years later, the exiles were allowed to go back to the homeland; however, my relatives chose to stay in Persia since they had established themselves there. After my parents died, my older cousin, Mordecai, adopted me and raised me to believe in the one true God.

Your story tells the circumstances that were essential to the survival of God's people in Persia. These circumstances were not the result of chance, but of God's design. Scripture tells us the King of Persia gave a banquet for all the princes and officials in his kingdom. This celebration was a tremendous display of wealth and glory of his empire. The banquet lasted six months and had become a drunken party by the time it finally ended. Will you tell us how you came to be involved in the happenings over the next few months?

As the all-male party and the drinking progressed, the drunken King called for Queen Vashti to parade her beauty before the drunken crowd. Knowing it would displease the King and might cost her life, Queen Vashti refused to go. The king was embarrassed and humiliated before his partygoers. He was so angry he made a law that Queen Vasthi be forever banished from the Kingdom. Included in the law was the statement that husbands everywhere would receive proper respect from their wives.

It is hard to believe the King would make a law demanding wives be required to show their husbands respect. I suppose he was unaware respect cannot be mandated by Law; it has to be earned. Esther, how did that involve you?

The king had a harem of young women; however, I suspect he began to miss the queen he had banished. His attendants determined to search the empire for beautiful, young virgins, hoping the king might find a queen among them. I was one of the young women brought to the king's harem. The King's eunuch, who was in charge of the girls, went out of his way to help me prepare to meet the king. Mordecai warned me I should not mention I was Jewish

We have read your story, and it seems the king was captivated by your beauty and fell in love with you at first sight. He set the royal crown on your head and declared you Queen. You were sent to live with his other wives. The rest of your story involves your cousin Mordecai. Tell us what happened next.

By this time, Mordecai had advanced to the position of palace guard. He overheard two of the king's eunuchs hatching a plot to assassinate the king. Mordecai informed me and I sent a message to the king telling about the plot. The two men were hanged on the gallows, and the deed was recorded in the history of King Xerxes's reign.

About that same time, the king promoted Haman to be prime minister. This made Haman the most powerful official in the empire. All in the kingdom were ordered to show respect by bowing before Haman. Mordecai refused to bow down to this wicked man. Haman was furious and devised a plan to get rid of Mordecai.

Haman talked the king into issuing an edict that people of the Jewish race who did not obey the laws of the land be destroyed. The king signed that decree without even reading it. Haman thought he had gotten his way, so he ordered a seven-and- half- foot gallows built on which to hang Mordecai.

Esther, why would Haman want to destroy all the Jews just because Mordecai would not bow down to him?

Haman was an Agagite, a descendant of Agag the king of the Amalekites. The Amalekites were ancient enemies of the Jews. In addition, Haman loved power and authority. He hated that Mordecai would not give him the reverence he felt was his due. His quest for personal power and his hatred of the Jewish race consumed him.

Scripture tells us that one night the king was unable to sleep and read the history of his reign. He read how Mordecai had saved his life by reporting a plot to assassinate him. The King felt he needed to honor Mordecai, so he asked his trusted advisor, Haman, how he could honor such a man. Haman, thinking the King meant to honor him said the man should ride throughout the kingdom wearing the King's robe and signet ring. Meanwhile, your own drama was taking place.

Mordecai urged me to go to the king, and ask him to rescind the edict to destroy the Jewish people. I knew the King could have me killed for coming to him without an invitation; however, Mordecai's words touched my heart. He said, "Who can say but that you have been elevated to the palace for just such a time as this?" I asked Mordecai to gather all the Jews together to fast and pray for me, and I would go in to see the King. I prepared a dinner for the King and Haman. That went well, so I invited them to a second dinner. At the second dinner, I revealed the plot Haman had put into motion. I asked the King to spare my life and the lives of my people.

You are a very brave woman. However, I am sure that knowing Mordecai and the people were fasting and praying for you gave you courage to approach the King without a summons. We know the King was receptive, probably because he loved you. When he heard your plea for the Jewish people, he ordered his attendants to hang Haman on the gallows he had built to hang Mordecai.

On the same day Haman was hanged and the King honored Mordecai, I shared with the King that Mordecai and I were cousins and of the Jewish race. The King held out the golden scepter to me, and I was able to come before him. I asked that he rescind the decree Haman had devised to kill all the Jews. Haman's decree stated that on a certain day he would set, anyone could kill the Jews and take their property. A king's decree could not be rescinded; however, the King gave Mordecai the authority to write a new law.

Esther, with God's help, you were instrumental in saving your whole race. What was the new decree the King made?

The King's decree gave the Jews in every city authority to unite and defend their lives. The King placed the royal robe and crown of gold on Mordecai, and the people of Persia celebrated. Many of the people of the land came to believe in the one true God, because they saw God had blessed us as a people.

* * *

While the name of God is not found in the book of Esther, we clearly see God at work in the lives of Esther and Mordecai. Because of Esther's courageous act, a whole nation was saved. She saw a God-given opportunity and seized it! Her life made a difference. Are you watching for God at work in your life? Perhaps He has prepared you to act in "such a time as this." God is in control and has a plan for each of our lives.

THOUGHTS FOR DISCUSSION FROM THE LIFE OF ESTHER

- Do you believe that God always has a purpose for situations in which He places us? Why or why not?

- Who is the hero in this story, Esther or Mordecai? Defend your choice.

- Esther wanted to make sure Mordecai and the people were fasting and praying for her as she went to the king. How do you feel about fasting? Is fasting necessary for a Christian? Share a time when you have felt the need to fast and pray.

- We may not be risking our lives as Esther did when she went to talk to the king, but how willing are we to talk to someone about Christ even if we know we might be laughed at or ridiculed?

- Esther was the right person at the right time at the right place. What about you? Could this be your "such a time as this"? Share your thoughts.

- Do you trust God to work in the events of your life for His glory and your best interests, even though you may not see the results at the time? What gives you that hope?

GOD'S UNCONDITIONAL LOVE (GOMER AND HOSEA)
BOOK OF HOSEA

We are privileged to have two guests with us today: Hosea and Gomer. Hosea, at the time your story began, you were a prophet to the northern kingdom of Israel. Israel was in one of those periods when they had turned from the one true God and adopted the moral behavior and idolatrous religion of the surrounding Canaanites. As a prophet, you had taken a vow to obey and serve God in any way possible. I am sure you never dreamed God would give you an assignment that would break your heart.

I never really questioned the assignments God gave me. With each assignment, I just determined to do my best to be worthy of my calling. Yes, this assignment did break my heart; however, it gave me a love beyond my deepest hope or expectations. I had been praying that God would bless me with a wife. Eventually, God said He was going to give me a wife, but it would not be the usual marriage. God was going to use my relationship with my wife to show the northern kingdom unless they repented of their sin and turned back to God, they would be destroyed.

I am sure you must have been shocked when you realized God was going to use your relationship with the woman you would marry to illustrate His relationship with Israel. God told you to marry a prostitute who would be unfaithful. That would be a hard thing to hear. Did you accept that assignment right away?

I will have to admit I did argue with God at first. I wanted to be sure that I had heard him right. It did not make sense to me. I was a prophet preaching His word, and He was telling me to marry a prostitute. However, God explained He was going to use my marriage to illustrate the way the Israelites were being untrue to Him. They were openly committing adultery against the Lord by worshiping other gods. I had been preaching the same message, so I saw the wisdom of using my marriage to call attention to the sins of the Israelites. *I had to obey God, even if it was against my desires, religious convictions, and moral standards. I knew people would ridicule me, but I had to trust God for the outcome. I really thought God would change His mind. God did not change His mind and I learned what it's like to love someone unconditionally. My experience helped me see the love God has for me.*

I understand Hosea, and I am sure you loved Gomer. The more you grew to love Gomer, the more you understood His love for His people. You began to understand why it was so important to God that Israel turn from their sin, and serve Him. Gomer, what were your feelings at this point?

Hosea was a nice man, and he was good to me. However, the life of a prophet is so restrictive. When our first child was born, God told Hosea to name him Jezreel. Hosea said it meant that God was going to punish King Jehu's dynasty. By this time, I was getting a little tired of the restrictions of being the wife of a prophet. Hosea was older than me, and even though it was fine when we were first married, I was still a young and beautiful, and I wanted to have fun. After a few years, I started going out alone.

Hosea, you probably thought that your life with Gomer would be better after the birth of your son. Instead, she began to be less and less interested in your ministry, and came to resent it. She accused you of caring more about your ministry than you did her. However, you had to obey God, so you went on preaching, calling for the northern kingdom to repent and turn back to the Lord. Your wife had other interests, and spent more time away from home. How did you handle her being away so much?

I spent a lot of time in prayer. It was obvious Gomer did not share my love for the Lord's work. Her absences away from our home became more frequent. You can imagine my shame and heartbreak. I lay awake at night wrestling with my fears, and I preached with a heavy heart. I was afraid she would take other lovers. I was sure she had done just that when she became pregnant again. I knew the baby was not mine. It was a beautiful little girl, and at God's direction, I named her Loruhama, which means unloved. Again, the name was symbolic of Israel's wanderings from God's love, and the discipline she would soon experience. However, nothing could soothe my troubled soul.

I cannot even imagine how you felt. Then almost immediately, Gomer was pregnant again. This time God directed you to call the child, Lo-ammi, which means "not my people." You knew for sure this baby was also not yours. You continued to preach prophecy describing Jehovah's relationship with His unfaithful Israel, and all the while, your own life was falling apart.

You cannot imagine the heartbreak. I tried reasoning with Gomer. I pleaded with her, and threatened to disinherit her. She continued to be with the men who lavished material things on her. A few times, she repented and came home, and her repentance never lasted.

Soon the final blow fell. Gomer, did you write a note, or send a message by a friend telling Hosea it was over for good this time? Could you not see that Hosea loved you? Could you not see how he was suffering? Hosea cared for you deeply and grieved for you as though you had died. I am sure his heart ached that you could choose a life that would surely bring you to ruin. His friends were probably thinking it was good riddance. However, Hosea did not feel that way. He longed to have you home. What do you have to say for yourself Gomer?

As I said, Hosea was a good man, but I just did not love him anymore. It was exciting to be with a different man every night. They wined me, bought me jewels, and told me how beautiful I was. I was not meant to be the wife of a prophet. All he did was go to church and pray, so I left. However, it was not long until I began to see how empty my life had become. There were too many men, and too much booze. Eventually, I hit bottom. My life was a blur, and one day I found myself on the auction block. I don't even know how I got there. Maybe that last man sold me into slavery. All my friends had deserted me, and I had no means of support.

In the meantime Hosea, you were living out the message you were preaching about God. Day after day, you reminded the Israelites of God's unconditional love for them. You accused them of committing spiritual adultery with false and

pagan idols, but you also told them of God's continuing love. As you spoke of God wanting to restore fellowship with his people, I am sure you were thinking of Gomer. We know eventually God told you to go and find Gomer and love her again. What were your feelings? Did you still love her?

I never stopped loving my wife, even though she was an adulterer. God told me to love her as He loved the Israelites, though they turned to other gods. I begun searching for her and found her on the auction block in a filthy slave market. I was not a wealthy man, but I bought her for fifteen shekels of silver and five bushels of barley. People made fun of me. They wanted to know why I would pay anything for that hag when they could get her for nothing. However, this was Gomer, the woman I loved. I paid the highest price anyone would pay. I knew that was the only way to restore her dignity. I took her by the hand and brought her to our home. At God's command, I did have to institute some restrictions on her to wean her away from her sinful lifestyle. Afterwards, she would be my wife again in every sense of the word.

Hosea, we can tell by the smiles on both your faces, that she was fully restored as your wife. The restrictions you placed on Gomer when she came back to you are representative of the restrictions God placed on Israel.

Gomer, you finally came to understand how much you were loved. God forgave you, cleansed your life, and gave you another chance. Hosea never gave up on you, just as God has never given up on Israel, and He never will. He has never given up on us, and He never will.

THOUGHTS FOR DISCUSSION FROM THE LIVES OF GOMER AND HOSEA

- How did Israel respond after God demonstrated His love by delivering them from Egyptian slavery and providing for their daily needs?

- What is the real message in the story of Gomer and Hosea? What title would you give this story?

- What are some ways that a person commits spiritual adultery?

- We may not commit adultery as Gomer did; however; today we are still chasing after other loves. Name some of the loves we chase after.

- Can churches commit spiritual adultery? What are some consequences for churches that are unfaithful?

- Hosea's love for Gomer was loyal, tender, and unchanging. He never gave up pursuing her. Did God pursue you the same way? Share your story.

- What were the restrictions or tough love Hosea imposed on Gomer?

- Israel is today experiencing "tough love" from God. Explain.

- When will the "tough love" end for Israel?

- Give an example of tough love God sometime uses on us.

THE STORY OF JEZEBEL
1 KINGS 31:2 KINGS 9:37

There was a good man called Naboth,
He was a real God-fearing man
And there was also a wicked king
Who wanted his little patch of land!

But Naboth wouldn't sell his vineyard.
He said, "There is just no way!"
God gave me that land,
And I am here to stay!

Wicked king became angry and sullen.
He pouted like a child.
He threw a great big tantrum
He was like a man gone wild!

Along comes his loving wife.
She was wicked same as he.
Upon hearing of his problem
She said, "Just leave it to me!"

She was up to no good,
Jezebel was her name.
And getting her own way

Was her favorite game.

So with manipulation and deceit
Jezebel got her way.
She brought in liars and thieves,
And poor Naboth died that day.

The land went to the king.
Hooray! They had won!
So celebrate they did
Wicked king and wicked one!

But looking down from heaven
God had seen it all.
He called on Elijah the prophet
To make this important call.

So here came the judge.
Elijah looked Ahab in the eye.
"You are doomed, my friend,
And it's way too late to cry!"

The dogs will lick your blood
You and the missus, too.
Your payday has come,
And there's nothing you can do!

Elijah's prophecy was fulfilled,
And it happened just that way
King Ahab was killed in battle
And the dogs had a heyday!

But what of the wicked Jezebel?
She continued for a while.
A new king came to town,
And she revved up her wiles.

She painted her face and fixed her hair
Piled on the jewels and such.
She planned to seduce the new king
But boy, was she out of touch!

The new king told her eunuchs
"Throw the wicked one down."
The dogs waited patiently below
Their supper they had found.

What a happy day in Jezreel!
Elijah's prophecy had come true
They had met their payday someday
Did wicked one and wicked two!

That's the end of the Jezebel story
And we shake our head and say
I'd never be like her,
But are we in some little way?

Are we ever strong willed and domineering?
Are we eager to take charge and then
We just keep going our own way
And don't recognize it as sin?

There may be a bit of Jezebel in each of us

The lesson from her life is clear.
Rejecting God brings disaster;
But loving Him leaves nothing to fear.

SECTION TWO

WOMEN OF THE NEW TESTAMENT

"In the past God spoke to our fore-fathers through the prophets at many times and in various ways, but in these last days He has spoken to us by His Son, whom He appointed heir of all things, and through whom He made the universe."

HEBREWS 1:1-2 NIV

CHOSEN BY GOD (MARY)
LUKE 1:26-38; MATTHEW
1:18-242:1-38; JOHN19:25-27

Mary, it is an honor to have you as our guest today. We know you grew up in a typical Jewish home in Nazareth where scriptures were taught. You knew the prophecy that a young, Jewish virgin would bear a son who would be the Savior of the world. Did you ever dream you might be that girl?

I knew the prophecy, and I thought it would be wonderful to be chosen to be the mother of God's Son. However, I did not have time to dwell on what might happen. Recently I had become engaged to a man called Joseph. I loved Joseph, and we were to be married when the betrothal period ended. One day, as I was watering my donkey, I heard someone speak my name. I thought at first it was my father, but I soon realized it was a voice I did not recognize. Then I saw a shimmering presence, a form of such beauty that it had to be an angel. I was confused and frightened. The angel quieted my fear and said I would bear a son who would be called Jesus, the Son of the Most High.

The presence of the angel must have frightened you. What were your first thoughts?

My first thought was, "I am so unworthy." I remembered the times I had rebelled against my parents, envied my cousins, and had impure thoughts. I never doubted what the angel said was true; however I wondered why God would choose me. The angel assured me God knew the secrets of my heart, and He did not expect perfection. He said the child would be human as well as holy, so that man could find his way back to God. I did not understand everything at the time, but I accepted what He was telling me. I asked how I could have a child since I had not known a man. He said that with God all things are possible. The angel said the power of the Most High would overshadow me, and I would be with child.

Even though you were frightened and did not understand all that was to take place, you told the angel you were the willing handmaiden of the Lord. You were accepting God's plan for your life. Tell us when you knew you were with child.

After speaking with the angel, I felt the presence of God overshadowing me and taking possession of my body. I felt a movement in my body, and as I pressed my hand to my stomach, I felt I was one with God. I knew the miracle had happened, and I was with child. God had touched me and kindled life within me!

That must have been an awesome experience. However, at the same time you must have been wondering how you would tell your mother, father, and Joseph what had just happened to you.

I just knew God would take care of it. I told my mother first. She stood there looking at me trying to take in all I said. I am sure it was hard for her to accept that I was unmarried and with child. It was different with my father. He knew the scriptures, and began praising the Lord that I was chosen to give birth to the Messiah. It was especially hard to tell Joseph what had happened to me. He knew the child was not his, and he could not accept what I was saying.

We could see how Joseph would be torn. He loved you and did not want to bring shame on you, so he intended to put you away privately. One night as he slept, God's messenger appeared to Joseph and confirmed your story. The angel told him to go ahead and take you as his wife for the Holy Spirit had conceived the child within you. Before your baby was born, you and Joseph had to go to Bethlehem. Tell us about that visit.

Yes, we did have to go to Bethlehem to register for the census. This was a busy time in Bethlehem, and we could not find a place to stay. Finally, an innkeeper allowed us to stay in the stable with the animals. My baby was born in that stable.

While you were treasuring your moments with your newborn son, God was revealing the birth of His son to shepherds in the fields. The Lord's glory surrounded them as the armies of heaven sang His birth announcement, "Glory to God in the highest and on earth, peace and goodwill to men." That was an extraordinary birth announcement! The shepherds left their flocks and rushed to Bethlehem to see this miracle. The word spread that the Messiah was born! Mary, you kept all these things in your heart and pondered them. We know there are several traditions after the birth of a Jewish baby. Will you tell us about those traditions?

There are three ceremonies soon after a baby's birth. On the eighth day, a baby is circumcised and named. The circumcision symbolized the Jews' separation from Gentiles and their unique relationship with God. At the Redemption of the firstborn, the child is bought back to God with an offering. The parents are acknowledging the child belongs to God. The third ceremony is the purification of the mother.

Even though this was God's Son, you and Joseph carried out these traditional ceremonies according to God's law. This was further evidence that Jesus did not come to do away with the law, but to fulfill it perfectly. Tell us about the first time you brought Jesus to the Temple for dedication.

As we came into the Temple, Simeon the priest met us and prophesied that people would either joyfully accept Jesus, or totally reject him. I grieved for the widespread rejection I knew He would face. However, I had to trust God to protect Him through whatever was to come. Jesus grew and we marveled at His wisdom. When He was twelve years old, we thought He was with friends as we left the temple; however, we soon found he was not with them. We went back and found Him in the Temple discussing deep question with the religious teachers. It was then I realized we must take our hands off this child, for He belonged to God. Jesus was a good son and we rejoiced at every report we heard of His teaching and healing ministry.

The time came when you knew He had made many enemies with His preaching. The religious leaders of the day just could not believe that He was the Son of God. They accused him of blasphemy, and determined to put Him to death. Tell us about the night in the Garden of Gethsemane.

Some women and I followed Jesus and His disciples to the Garden where He went to pray. Jesus knew He was facing betrayal and death. We heard His agonizing prayer as He asked the Father to take the cup of suffering from Him. However, we knew, more than anything, Jesus wanted to do the Father's will, so we were not surprised His next prayer was, "Nevertheless, not my will, but thine be done." My heart ached. We watched as Judas came and greeted him with a kiss. I wanted to yell, "Son, run, run for your life," but the women constrained me. I knew this had been God's plan from the beginning. However, I did not know it would hurt so much. The women and I attended every trial and were overwhelmed when we heard the verdict. They were going to crucify the Son of God! My heart was breaking but even then, I felt the Holy Spirit comforting me, reminding me again this was part of God's master plan for mankind.

Mary, I know you were there as they nailed Him to the cross. As His disciples deserted Him, you and the other women who loved Him kept a vigil at the foot of the cross. Your heart must have been breaking as you listened to the trials and watched the crucifixion.

I cannot put into words how I felt knowing my child was going to experience such a horrible death. What hurt most was to know that it was my sins, along with the sins of humankind, that nailed Him to the cross. Then I heard Him say, "Father, forgive them, for they do not know what they do." The physical agony He experienced was horrible; however, even worse was the spiritual separation from His Father. Jesus was the perfect sacrifice to pay the penalty for man's sin. As a mother, I wondered why it had to be so.

Mary, I cannot imagine what it is like to lose a child. I know it must have comforted you to know in His last moments He thought of you, the mother who had loved Him and raised Him. He told John, "Behold your mother." Then His last words were, "Father, into your hands I commit my spirit." He breathed His last breath with full assurance of His Father's trustworthiness.

* * *

As Jesus hung on that cross, darkness filled the earth as the Light of the World was extinguished. We can rejoice today because the darkness is lifted and Mary's son, Jesus Christ, is alive! Praise God, He is alive, and we will be with Him in eternity. What an awesome God we serve!

THOUGHTS FOR DISCUSSION
FROM THE LIFE OF MARY,
MOTHER OF JESUS

- Mary and Joseph believed God and responded with obedience. How willing are you to accept the unique task He may be calling you to do?

- The privilege of being chosen to be the mother of God's Son caused Mary to have to deal with the stigma of being an unwed mother. Discuss the difference in how the word in Mary's day looked at unwed mothers and how we look at unwed mothers today.

- Why was the virgin birth crucial to Christianity?

- What unique problems do you think Mary had to deal with being the mother of Jesus?

- What are your feelings about those who outwardly express their feelings in the worship service, i.e., raising hands, saying amen, etc?

- There were at least three incidents in Mary's life that identified her life. She was chosen by God to give birth to His Son, she watched the crucifixion, and the resurrection of her son. Can you name three incidents that have shaped your life?

GOD NEVER FORGETS THE
FAITHFUL (ELIZABETH)
LUKE 1:39-45, 57-80

Our guest today is described in the Bible as a woman "righteous before God, walking in all the commandments and ordnances of the Lord blameless." What a great description! Elizabeth, we are so glad to have you here. Will you tell us a little about yourself?

There is really not much to tell. I live in the country of Judea, about four miles south of Jerusalem. One of my ancestors was Aaron, the priest, and I married a priest. My husband Zacharias, served in the Temple, and I spent my days making sure he looked nice and his priestly vestments were in good repair. I also acted as host for Temple visitors. We were happy; however, as we grew older our one regret was God had never blessed us with children.

It sounds as if you had a good life serving the Lord. However, things were about to change for you. Tell us about the time Zacharias came from his duties at the Temple and could not speak. That must have been frightening for both of you.

Yes, it was very scary, but I noticed he had a smile on his face. I knew it could not be too bad or he would not have had that silly grin on his face. It took some time for him to make me understand that Gabriel, God's angel, had appeared to him.

Gabriel announced I would bear a child that would be filled with the Holy Ghost from his mother's womb.

Did you find it hard to believe what Zacharias was telling you? After you had longed for a child all these years and had probably given up hope, Zacharias was telling you that you were going to have a child. Did you believe what he was saying, or did you think, "It's not going to happen at my age"?

I did have a few moments of alarm. I wondered if I was too old to have a child. I worried that Zacharias's muteness was not from wonder, but from fear for the greater disappointment that awaited us. God's miracle would prove to be a mockery if I delivered a stillborn child. However, I had always believed in miracles, so now I chose to believe in my God who is able to do anything He says He will do. Therefore, I put all the negative thoughts aside and received the news with joy and thanksgiving. Finally, God was going to bless me with an answer to my prayer! I felt a great sense of humility and reverent responsibility. I praised God for His goodness and mercy to us, and thanked Him for His promise.

I know when you were about six months pregnant; you had a very special visitor. Will you tell us about that visit?

One evening as I was dreaming about the baby God had promised, I had a strange sense of anticipation. It was a premonition, or a strong conviction that something important was about to happen. There was a knock at my door. When I opened the door, my young niece Mary, was standing there. I was surprised to see she was also expecting a child. At the sound of Mary's voice, I felt my baby move within me.

Elizabeth, you immediately recognized the baby Mary was carrying as the Messiah. Apparently, the Holy Spirit had prepared you for this visit; for you greeted her as the mother of the Lord and told her what an honor it was to have her visit you. Your greeting must have strengthened Mary's faith. She probably was finding it hard to believe all that had happened to her and needed your wise council.

Mary was so young. I cannot even imagine how she could comprehend all that happened to her. What an honor to be chosen to be the mother of God's son! She was feeling unworthy and overwhelmed with the responsibility; however, Mary's first words to me did not reflect any hesitation in accepting the role God had chosen for her. We rejoiced together in being used of God in such a marvelous way.

We know that God had already revealed to you that your expected child would be the messenger preparing the way for the Messiah. I am not surprised Mary came to you at this time. Even though you were pregnant with a long-awaited son, you could have envied Mary because her son would be greater than your son.

I had no reason to envy Mary. I was thrilled Mary's son would be the long-awaited Messiah and my son would announce His coming. I was filled with joy that Mary came to me and we rejoiced together.

I am sure Mary was a great help to you as you experienced the discomforts of a first pregnancy in old age. Mary stayed with you about three months and then returned home. Shortly after Mary's visit, your son was born. Tell us about his birth.

Yes, my son was born, and I treasured every moment with awe. On his eighth day, true to Jewish tradition, relatives and neighbors gathered for the circumcision and naming of my child. Some of those present called him Zacharias after his father, but I remembered what the angel had said. Therefore, I told them his name would be John. They looked to Zacharias for approval. When he nodded his affirmation, his tongue was loosed, and he could speak again. What a joyful moment that was; my husband could speak again, and I had a son to be used by God.

We know from scriptures your son was different. From birth, he was set apart as a Nazirite – one set apart for God's service. John remained faithful to that calling all the days of his life. He lived in the wilderness until God's word of direction came to him. He wore strange clothes and ate strange food. He had no prestige or power in the Jewish political system; however, he spoke with authority. Even as people crowded to him because of his message, he always pointed them to Jesus, never forgetting his role as messenger for the Son of God.

Yes, he was different from most people. However, I had taught him from the beginning to follow God's plan for his life. He did that, and I was very proud of my son.

* * *

As Elizabeth and Mary visited about their coming sons during the three months they were together, could they have known, or had a premonition of what the future held for them and their sons? Elizabeth's son, John the Baptist, would eventually be beheaded by Herod, ruler of Galilee.

Mary's son would be crucified on the cross by an angry mob and die for our sins. I will leave you to speculate whether or not either mother would have changed things if they could have done so. I am sure Elizabeth the mother of John, found comfort in the words of Christ when He said, "Verily I say unto you, among them that are born of women, there hath not risen one greater than John the Baptist." What a tribute to a gracious, godly woman: Elizabeth, the mother of John.

THOUGHTS FOR DISCUSSION
FROM THE LIFE OF ELIZABETH

- Luke describes Elizabeth as a woman who was "righteous before God." What does it mean for a person to be righteous before God?

- Elizabeth and Zacharias's commitment and dedication to God was not based on what He had or had not done for them, but their love for Him. On what do you base your commitment and dedication?

- Do you sometimes lose hope when things do not happen according to your schedule? What might God be trying to do by delaying His answer?

- God blessed Elizabeth for her vital role in raising John. Do you consider bringing up your children a God-given ministry for you or the church?

- Elizabeth was older than Mary; however, God chose her to affirm and encourage Mary. Tell of some older person who has mentored or encouraged you. Have you ever mentored a younger person?

- As Elizabeth and Mary awaited their sons' births, what do you think they discussed? Do you see any evidence that they understood the impact their sons would make on the redemption of the world?

- How can women today have a part in God's plan as they raise their own children to live for the Lord?

GOD'S FAITHFUL
WITNESS (ANNA)
LUKE 2:36–38

Today we have a remarkable woman with us—one of the first people in Israel to recognize Jesus as the Messiah. Even though many of the faithful believers in Israel were eagerly awaiting the Messiah and looking diligently for Him, they failed to recognize Him. The only people who did recognize Christ at His birth were humble people like our visitor today. I would like you to meet Anna, who is described in the Bible as a prophet. Anna, did you predict the future? Exactly, what does it mean to be a prophet?

A prophet is not a fortuneteller. The main role of a prophet is to speak for God and proclaim His truth. My ministry was offering words of encouragement and instruction from Hebrew Scripture to the women who came to the temple to worship.

Anna, just the fact that you are referred to as a prophet is unique. Only five women in the Old Testament and you and one other in the New Testament were referred to as prophets in the Scriptures. We know you were the daughter of Phanuel of the tribe of Asher, who belonged to the apostate northern kingdom of Israel. You were raised in a pagan atmosphere, but your family was a part of the believing remnant from the northern kingdom. You are truly a living example of God's faithfulness to His people. **Tell us a little about yourself, and how you came to live in the Temple.**

I was married when I was very young. After seven years of marriage, my husband died, and I never remarried. Widowhood was extremely difficult in my day, and virtually guaranteed a life of extreme poverty. I went to live on the Temple grounds and served as a caretaker. I was allowed to stay on the grounds even after I could no longer work as a caretaker. I spent my time fasting and praying night and day.

It is obvious you are a most extraordinary woman. You lived the simplest kind of life in the Temple, and could always be found fasting and praying. Fasting reveals a heart so consumed with praying, and so eager to receive the blessing being sought, the person simply has no interest in eating. Anna, what was the focus of your prayers?

I prayed with the women who came to the Temple. However, my focus was praying and fasting for the coming of the Messiah. I taught prophecy for many years, and I never once doubted that one day those prophecies would be fulfilled. God had promised He would send the Messiah and I looked forward to that time.

Anna, your faith is amazing! While others had given up hope of the Messiah coming to deliver them, your faith carried you through sixty-four years of watching, waiting, and praying for prophecy to be fulfilled. You believed the Prophet Isaiah when He said, "Behold a king shall reign in righteousness." Finally, after all those years of waiting, your faith was rewarded, and God allowed you to see these prophecies fulfilled.

For years, I had searched the skies for evidence of the Messiah's appearing. This particular night I saw the star in the east, and my heart quickened within me. I knew instantly God was telling me my waiting had not been in vain. Christ was born that night. I did not know where the Messiah was born, but I knew the time had come when I would finally see Him with my own eyes. I was overcome with joy.

You did get to see the Messiah forty days later when his parents brought Him to the Temple for the ceremonial service of His mother's purification. Tell us about that visit.

I watched as the little family brought the baby Jesus to the Temple. By the providence of God, I was within earshot of Simeon, the priest, who was blessing the child. By faith, I knew everything for which I had been praying and fasting was right there in the arms of Simeon. God answered my prayers; I was seeing the Messiah at last!

Anna, as Joseph and Mary quietly made their way out of the Temple with the child Jesus that day, we can imagine you unobtrusively returning to your thanksgiving and prayer in the Temple. I cannot even begin to imagine how you felt seeing the long-awaited Christ child. Scripture tells us your prophetic gift came boldly to the forefront and you spoke of Him to all who were searching for redemption.

I could do nothing else. God had answered my prayers in a most blessed way. He had allowed me to be one of the first to see the redeemer of Israel in the flesh. I sought out the believing remnant, and spoke to them about Him at every opportunity. I knew, at my age, I would not be around when He began His ministry. However, that did not matter. I had seen the Messiah, the fulfillment of the scriptures I had taught!

* * *

The day of His dedication was probably the one and only glimpse Anna had of the Messiah. Anna did not live to witness the public manifestation of the Christ, or hear His divine teaching and promises. However, she had been there to behold Him, to thank God for Him, and to speak of Him to all those who had looked for the redemption He was to bring. The legacy Anna leaves is one of complete devotion to her Lord.

THOUGHTS FOR DISCUSSION
FROM THE LIFE OF ANNA

- Anna is described as a prophet. What do you see as the duties of a prophet?

- Anna was an elderly widow who lived in the Temple and served God with fasting and prayers. What was the purpose of her fasting?

- Does fasting have a place in your worshipping God? Explain.

- Along with the shepherds and a few other humble, remarkable people, Anna was among those few who did recognize Christ as the Messiah. What was the first thing Anna and the shepherds did when they saw Jesus? What was the first thing you did when you met Jesus?

- Anna's life is an example of how the elderly can serve the Lord. Tell about a modern-day Anna you know.

- Are you willing to spend your latter years mentoring and encouraging others?

- Anna only caught a glimpse of the Christ child. As we search our hearts, have we caught a glimpse of what we can be if we dedicate our lives to Him as Anna did?

- Anna's legacy was one of fasting and prayer. What is your legacy?

TOO LITTLE, TOO LATE
MATTHEW 27:15-26

Today we have with us the distinguished wife of Pontius Pilate. There is no mention of her name in scripture; however, tradition has called her Claudia. Therefore, for the purpose of this interview, we will call her Claudia.

Claudia, we know your husband was Roman Governor of Judea, and there was a mutual hatred between Pilate and the Jewish people.

I think that may have been the reason the Romans chose him to be Governor. His job depended on keeping peace in Judea. It was not an easy task, especially during the time of great festivals when the city was overrun with people coming to worship at the Temple.

Some have called your husband cruel and oppressive. Pilate was a very political man, and would do anything to capture the attention of his superiors in Rome. This was a particularly uneasy time in Judea. This man, Jesus, had been arrested, and the mob was calling for his death. This must have caused Pilate some concern.

Rebellion was a constant threat during a time such as this. I was especially concerned because on my many trips to Jerusalem, I had become aware of this man Jesus. I had observed the miracles He had performed, and had been impressed with His ministry to the common people. I wanted to know more about

Him; however, I knew my husband would not approve. Pilate's lack of concern for the Jewish people was well known, and I am sure he saw Jesus of Nazareth as a potential rebel who must be taken care of as quickly as possible.

You held the highest position of any woman in Palestine, but we sense a tender and gentle nature as you tried to temper your husband's violence with your growing concern for the Jewish people. Tell us how you found yourself in the middle of the trial of Jesus.

The Jewish leaders had to persuade the Roman government to sentence Jesus to death because they did not have the authority to do it themselves. They wanted the death to be Roman-sponsored so the crowds could not blame them. The Jewish leaders had arrested Jesus for blasphemy, which did not carry a death penalty. He had claimed to be king; therefore, they could charge Him for being a threat to Caesar. He was taken to Ananias, then to Caiaphas, and finally they brought Him to stand before my husband.

For a leader who was supposed to administer justice, Pilate seemed to be more concerned with political expediency than doing the right thing. He had several opportunities to make the right decision. He was amazed that Jesus did not try to defend himself against the charges brought against Him. Pilate was smart enough to recognize the obvious plot against Jesus. Maybe he thought he had an out, since every year the custom was for the Governor to release one prisoner during the Passover celebration. Claudia, your woman's intuition probably made you sense impending evil. You wanted to save your husband from his terrible decision to put a just man to death, but the mob was strong and loud, and your husband was afraid of the mob.

It did hurt when there seemed to be nothing I could do that would change my husband's mind. I was afraid, because I had a dream the night before, and God revealed to me Jesus was an innocent man. My husband was sitting on the judgment seat, and was about to announce whether this just man would live or die. My husband had often asked my opinion on some important matter; therefore, I took the chance that he would listen to me now. I sent a note by a servant telling him of my dream and begging him not to condemn this righteous man.

It must have taken a great deal of courage to send that message while he was discharging his duties in a public place. Your voice was not strong enough to overcome the mob calling for the death of Jesus. Pilate did not recognize your message as a second chance from God. However, your message must have caused some concern for Pilate, for he asked the crowd a second time whom he should release. They continued to cry for the release of Barabbas and the crucifixion of Jesus. He stood before the crowd, washed his hands, and cried out, "I am innocent of the blood of this man; the responsibility is yours!" Although Pilate made the decision to let the crowd crucify Jesus, his guilt remained. Claudia, I am sure God knows you did all you could do at that time.

Yes, I tried; but it was too little, too late. As God spoke to me in that dream, I realized the traditions, rituals, and beliefs of the Roman pagan gods were false. Perhaps, if I had realized that sooner, I may have been able to convince my husband of the innocence of Jesus.

Many times when we read the story of the crucifixion of Jesus, we overlook your words to your husband. However, your act of speaking out regardless of the consequences, is a reminder to us we are to speak out when God convicts us to do so, whether or not we see results. The results are in God's hands.

* * *

The note sent by his wife did not stop Pilate from allowing the crucifixion of Jesus. However, she did what God had put on her heart, and we commend her for that. The lessons from the wife's life speak volumes to us. Evidently, Pilate had never heard anything definite about Jesus until that night. The whole incident was new, troublesome, and difficult for him. Had his wife begun sharing her feelings before that night, she might have convinced her husband of the innocence of Jesus. However, she had not, and her note was nothing more than an interruption. Perhaps her lifestyle did not reflect the message she was trying to convey to Pilate. It was too little, too late.

THOUGHTS FOR DISCUSSION
FROM THE LIFE OF THE
WIFE OF PONTIUS PILATE

- Some have said that Pilate's wife's dream could not have been from God because God sent Jesus to die for our sins. Give arguments supporting your view.

- From what little we know of her life, do you think she was already a believer, or was the dream a conversion experience?

- Since a wife can have a great influence on her husband, why do you think Pilate's wife failed in that area? On the other hand, did she fail completely?

- The one and only advocate to speak up for the legally and morally innocent Jesus was a woman who was a foreigner and an enemy. What does this say to you about the place of women in the church?

- What are some special gifts that women bring to the church?

- Do you think God speaks to us through dreams today? Has He ever spoken to you through a dream? If so, explain.

- If she had succeeded in convincing Pilate to pardon Jesus, do you think humanity would have remained unredeemed? What might have happened?

SHE DARED TO ASK A FAVOR OF JESUS (MOTHER OF JAMES AND JOHN)
MATTHEW 20:20–28, LUKE 9:51-56

Today we meet another amazing woman of the Bible. We are not even sure of her name. However, we do know she was the wife of Zebedee, and the mother of two famous sons. James and John were among the first disciples chosen to follow Jesus. This mother also became a devoted follower of Christ. She is thought to be one of the women who stood at the cross witnessing the crucifixion of Jesus, and at the tomb to hear the angel announce the glorious resurrection of Jesus.

Welcome, Mrs. Zebedee. I have always been intrigued by the name given your sons. Will you tell us how they came to be known as the Sons of Thunder?

I think they were given that name because they were always where the action was, and usually they were the ones causing the action. For example, as Jesus and His disciples made their way to Jerusalem for the Passover, my sons went on ahead to prepare the way for Jesus. They came to one Samaritan village where the people refused to welcome Jesus. This angered James and John, and they asked Jesus if they could call down fire from heaven to consume the village. Of course, Jesus rebuked them.

After the ascension of Jesus, Christianity began to spread through the villages of Samaria. When this happened, James and John were sent by the church in Jerusalem to minister to all these new believers in Samaria. I cannot even imagine how they felt to see this village full of new Christians; the very place that years earlier their temper had made them want to destroy.

With all their faults, they wanted the best for Jesus. Another incident that probably earned them the name, Sons of Thunder, happened when James and John found a man using Jesus' name to cast out demons. They were probably a little jealous of a man who healed in Jesus' name. They seemed more concerned about their own group's position, than in helping to free those troubled by demons. They thought they were protecting Jesus, but He rebuked them again.

We can understand James and John's concern. We do the same thing today when we refuse to associate with Christians from other denominations because they have different methods of winning people to Christ. James and John were living up to their name of Sons of Thunder.

I will be the first to admit they were not perfect, but they are my sons, and I wanted the best for them. With all their faults, Jesus loved them. My youngest son, John probably was the disciple who most nearly expressed the Spirit of Jesus. John was with Jesus at the wedding in Cana, and at the raising of Jairus' daughter. He was there in the Garden of Gethsemane, and the Transfiguration of Jesus. John was given the place of honor seated next to Jesus at the Last Supper. Because of his deep spiritual insight and loving disposition, Jesus loved John greatly, and entrusted his own mother to him at the end.

You must be a very proud mother. Tell us a little about James.

James, my oldest son was also a faithful disciple. He witnessed the life, ministry, death, and resurrection of Jesus. He, along with his brother, was at Jesus' side for the glory of the Transfiguration, and the agony in the garden of Gethsemane.

Mrs. Zebedee, you are a typical mother who is proud and ambitious for your sons. Will you tell us about the time you asked a favor of our Lord?

Yes, I knew my sons were outstanding men. They were not like Peter, who was just a common fisherman, or Matthew, the Roman tax collector, and they surely were much better and more qualified than Judas Iscariot. Why shouldn't they have the privilege of ruling with Jesus when He came into His Kingdom? Of course, the other disciples were jealous; they also wanted that special privilege. They thought I had made a selfish request, but I felt comfortable going to Jesus for my sons.

How wonderful that you felt comfortable, and had enough confidence in the love of Jesus, to ask that your sons be granted the honor of sitting one on His right hand, and the other on the left when He came into His Kingdom. You were presumptuous enough to put your own human ambition for your sons above everything. Will you tell us about Jesus' reaction to your request?

Jesus spoke kindly to me and said, "To sit on my right hand and on my left is not mine to give, but it shall be given to them for whom it is prepared of my Father." I wish He had stopped there. However, I probably needed Jesus' tender rebuke in order to realize that true spiritual greatness is not a thing to be given, but to be earned, and it can only be earned through sacrifice. Jesus then explained the definition of true greatness; "Whosoever will be great among you, let him be your minister." I learned much that day.

* * *

Mrs. Zebedee was a proud mother and she had every reason to be proud. Her sons were passionate men who loved and followed Jesus. Which one of us could say we would not have asked the same for our children? However, we cannot help but see the striking contrast of this mother and the mother of Jesus. Mary never expressed any human ambition for her son. Even when great things were spoken to her about her son, she "pondered these things in her heart."

TOUGHTS FOR DISCUSSION
FROM THE LIFE OF THE
MOTHER OF JAMES AND JOHN

- It is easy to think, "What was she thinking asking such a request of Jesus?" Would you have asked the same question of Jesus for your child? Why or why not?

- She knew the scriptures; however, do you think she fully understood what she was asking of Jesus? Was she talking about an earthly kingdom or spiritual kingdom?

- What lesson did Jesus teach her and her sons about how to be great in the Kingdom of God?

- Most mothers are naturally proud of their sons and want to see them promoted and honored. What is the danger you see in such a request?

- Jesus rebuked James and John for condemning the man who was speaking in Jesus' name. Why would they want to stop someone from teaching about Jesus?

- Give an instance where this may happen in today's world.

- One of her sons stood by Jesus during the crucifixion; one turned and ran. Which one stayed with Jesus, and which one deserted Him?

- What legacy did the mother of James and John leave for her sons?

DISTRACTED SERVANT AND DEDICATED SERVICE (MARY AND MARTHA)
MATTHEW 26:6–13, Luke 10:38–42; JOHN 11:1–45

Welcome Mary and Martha. We have read about you in the scriptures, and it is a privilege to have you both with us today. Mary, we will start with you. We know from Scriptures that you lived in Bethany, along with your sister, Martha, and your brother, Lazarus. Jesus came to your home often. He must have felt welcome there. Would you tell us about an incident that happened during one of His visits?

Jesus was always welcome in our home. We loved Him, and did what we could to support His ministry. This particular incident happened as Jesus was sharing with the disciples what would happen after the Passover. He said He would be betrayed and crucified. I was overcome with emotion, and my only thought was to show Him how much I loved Him. I took my most prized possession an alabaster box filled with perfume, and anointed His feet.

Mary, that was a beautiful thing to do, but not everyone agreed. I understand His disciples thought it was a waste of the oil that could have been sold, and the money given to the poor. I am sure Jesus understood what you did. What did Jesus say to the disciples?

He stated they would always have the poor with them, but that I had anointed Him for His burial. At the time, I did not fully understand what He was saying, and neither did the disciples. I just wanted to give the best I had to my Savior to try to show know how much I loved Him.

I am sure He was pleased with your offering. Martha, will you tell us about another time Jesus came to your home?

I was always thrilled to have Jesus visit our home. He was like part of our family. I love to entertain, so on this particular day, I was preparing a feast for Him. I wanted everything to be perfect. I had cleaned house all morning alone, and then I made homemade bread, cooked a leg of lamb, and I—

Martha, Martha, you are making me hungry. I am sure you are a wonderful cook. What happened when Jesus arrived?

As usual, my sister was certainly no help in the kitchen. I was slaving away getting dinner ready and trying to make everything perfect for Jesus, but she just sat at His feet hanging on every word He said. I could have used her help, so I went to Jesus and asked if He could not see that I needed her help in the kitchen. I will have to admit I was stressed out, and maybe just a little jealous that Mary could be with Jesus while I was in the kitchen trying to get everything ready for the feast.

I understand Jesus rebuked you a little. How did you feel about that?

I was angry at first; however, after I thought about it a while, I decided I did deserve it. He pointed out to me that I was causing my own stress, because I was worried about doing "things," while Mary had chosen to spend her time listening and worshipping the Lord.

WOMEN OF THE BIBLE

How like Jesus! He was not condemning you for your unselfish service, and praising Mary for her loving worship. He was reminding you the most important priority in life is to love and worship Him.

Yes, I finally came to understand we all have different ways of expressing our love for Him. Mary and I have different talents, but He loves both of us.

You are not alone. At times, I think we all become so concerned with doing things for Him, we begin to neglect hearing Him and remembering what He has done for us. We sometimes allow our service for Christ to crowd out our worship of Him.

My sister would never do that. I have come to recognize He is the Son of God, and my whole duty in life is to glorify Him. I have learned a lot about worship from my sister Mary.

Mary, let us talk about the tine your brother was sick. You knew that Jesus would be risking His life by coming back to Judea; however, you knew how much He loved your brother, so you contacted Him anyway. You must have been disappointed that He did not come right away.

I did contact Jesus, and I was just a little disappointed that He did not come in time to save my brother. However, I knew in my heart that Jesus knew best and had a reason for not coming sooner. I did not fully understand then, but I came to realize that His delay was in God's timing. At times, I have thought He was not answering my prayers when He did not answer right away. However, I have learned that Jesus always meets our needs according to His perfect schedule and purpose. It is hard to be patient at a time like this.

140

Martha, when He did come, I understand you rushed out to meet Him, and told Him your brother had died, and was already in the grave. Jesus told you that your brother would rise again. Did you believe your brother would rise again?

Of course, I knew he would rise at the resurrection, but that was not what Jesus meant... He asked me if I believed that those who died believing in Him would live again. I assured Him I had always believed He was the Son of God, and could do anything. At this moment, I believed He was going to raise Lazareth from the dead, so I called Mary to come see Jesus.

Mary, when you saw Jesus, you fell down at His feet and began to weep. He saw you and the others weeping, and He wept openly. Isn't it great we have a God who cares, who weeps with us, and comforts us as only He can? He told the others to roll the stone away from the burial cave. What happened next?

You know Martha. She never thinks before she speaks. She should have known Jesus knew what He was doing. However, she informed Him, "Maybe you shouldn't roll that stone away because by now the smell will be terrible because he has been dead for four days." Can you imagine her trying to tell our Lord what to do? Jesus very patiently said to her, "Did I not tell you that if you believed, you would see the glory of God?"

They rolled the stone away, and Jesus looked up to heaven and thanked God for hearing His prayer. Then Jesus shouted, "Lazarus, come out!" Lazarus came out, bound in grave clothes with his face wrapped in a head cloth. Jesus told them, "Unwrap him and let him go!"

* * *

We are told many of the people who witnessed this miracle believed in Jesus. This incident was the last straw for the priests and Pharisees. They called the high council together and began to plot against Jesus. Caiaphas, the high priest said, "Why should the whole nation be destroyed? Let this one man die for the people." Isn't it amazing? Caiaphas was used by God to explain Jesus' death, even though he did not realize what he was doing. Jesus did die for the people, but it was to pay the penalty for sin of all humanity.

*

THOUGHTS FOR DISCUSSION FROM THE LIVES OF MARY AND MARTHA

- Do you think Martha's feelings about her sister were natural and understandable? Why or why not?

- Martha had good intentions. Can good intentions lead to bad behavior? What might have been a better way for Martha to handle her frustrations rather than going to Jesus?

- What evidences of pride and self-centeredness do you see in Martha's actions?

- What reasons did Mary have for anointing Jesus' head and worshiping at His feet at this time?

- What can we learn about the temperament of these two sisters from the way they reacted to their brother's death and burial?

- In what ways do Martha and Mary show contrast between doing good works and having faith?

- What kind of hospitality does Jesus receive in your life? Are you so busy serving God that you do not have time to know Him personally?

A WOMAN WITH OBSTINATE FAITH (THE SYROPHOENICIAN WOMAN)
MATTHEW 15:21–28

I especially wanted you to meet our visitor for today because her faith is a lesson for us. The Bible does not mention her name, but I am going to call her Faith. Faith is an appropriate name, because it was her faith that kept her going back to Jesus for the healing of her daughter. Most of us would have given up after the first rebuke from Jesus.

Faith, tell us something about yourself, and why you went to Jesus with your request.

My daughter was possessed by a demon, and I had heard of the miracles performed by this man Jesus. I determined to ask Him to heal my daughter. I realized Jesus might not have anything to do with me because I was from Canaan. However, I was desperate, so I came anyway.

We know the first time you asked Jesus to heal your daughter, He did not reply. However, the disciples had much to say. They asked Jesus to get rid of you because you were bothering them with your persistent begging. You were certainly focused on your mission, for you did not even look at them. It was Jesus you came to see, not the disciples. Tell us what happened next.

Jesus did not ask me to leave, but He did say He was sent only to help the people of Israel – God's lost sheep – not the Gentiles. I knew my place, but I was there asking for mercy. I knew since I was not part of the covenant of promise to the Jewish people, I did not have any right to ask for favors. However, I could not give up, so I just continued to beg Him to help me.

Faith, Jesus was telling you the Jews would have the first opportunity to accept Him as the Messiah because God wanted them to present the message of salvation to the rest of the world. Jesus was not rejecting you because you were a Gentile woman. He may have wanted to test your faith, or He may have wanted to use the situation as another opportunity to teach faith is available to all people. How did you feel when Jesus said that it was not right to take food from the children and throw it to the dogs? Were you offended when He likened you to a dog?

I could not afford to be offended. I knew dog was the term Jews commonly called Gentiles because they considered a dog more likely to accept God's blessing than a Gentile. I really did not care what He called me. I knew I was not worthy of even a loaf of bread, but I would settle for the crumbs that fell from the table. I reminded Jesus even dogs eat crumbs that fall from the master's table. I was begging for His mercy in the healing of my daughter. Because I knew of His compassion and love for all people, I felt He was using the term dog to contrast the way people felt about the Gentiles.

You knelt before Him again, and cried out for Him to help you. That must have greatly impressed our Savior. You were letting Him know you were aware of the plenty being lavished upon the people of Israel, and all that you were asking was for was a crumb that might fall to the floor. Your obstinate faith had its reward. Jesus commended you for your faith, granted your request, and your daughter was healed instantly. I am sure you never stopped praising Jesus.

* * *

Isn't it ironic that many Jews would lose God's blessing and salvation because they rejected Jesus, and many Gentiles would find salvation because they recognized and accepted Him?

THOUGHTS FOR DISCUSSION FROM THE LIFE OF THE SYROPHOENICIAN WOMAN

- What were your thoughts when Jesus first seemed to ignore the woman? What could have been His motive?

- Could He have been testing the woman's faith as He did sometimes with His disciples? Was He using this as another opportunity to teach that faith is available to all people?

- This woman was desperate. The disciples asked Jesus to get rid of her. Do you think it is possible to become so occupied with spiritual matters that we become oblivious to the needs around us? Has this happened in your church?

- Is this more apt to be true if the one in need is of another race? Give examples.

- Jesus commended the woman for her great faith. Why or why not would the delay in Jesus answering her request increase her faith?

- Does God delay answering our prayers at times until we are properly prepared to receive the blessing? Give examples.

A WAYWARD WOMAN
AND A WAITING SAVIOR
(WOMAN AT THE WELL)
JOHN 4:4–42

Our visitor today has requested we not identify her by name because she came from a very sordid background. Therefore, we are going to refer to her as Samantha. The incident we are going to talk about happened at Jacob's well in Samaria. Will you tell us why you happened to be there and what happened?

As you know, I am from Samaria. Samaritans are a mixed race of people descending from pagans who intermarried with the Israelites after the Assyrians conquered the northern kingdom. Jews consider us unclean, and would travel miles out of their way to keep from even going through our town on their way to Galilee. I chose to go to the well at noon so I would not encounter any of the women of the town. Let's just say they did not understand my lifestyle.

Samantha, there were several unusual things about the time you went to the well by yourself this particular day. There you saw a Jewish man sitting alone. He seemed to be waiting for you, but you did not know Him. I am sure you wondered why a Jewish man would speak to you, a Samaritan and a woman.

Yes, I am used to people looking the other way when they see me; however, this Jewish man looked straight at me and asked if I would give Him a drink of water. My first thought was, "What does He have in mind?" I could see He had no way to draw water. I was confused because His request was not rude. I was curious why He would even look at someone like me; much less ask me for a drink of water. Therefore, I asked Him, "Why would you, a Jew, ask a drink of me, a Samaritan woman?"

I suppose you were surprised by his answer. He said, "If you knew the gift of God, and who it is that asks for a drink, you would have asked Him for living water." I am sure that must have got your attention.

It sure did. At first, I wondered if He was like other men, and was just trying to pick me up. However, He sure did not look like that sort of man. When He spoke of living water I decided He must be some kind of rabbi or spiritual leader. I had never heard of such thing as living water, so I asked Him where I could get that kind of water. He did not answer, so I chided Him a bit. I asked if He thought He was greater than Jacob who gave us this well. I told Him there is no better water than what comes from this well.

Jesus was very patient with you, wasn't He? He explained that our bodies thirst and need drinking water, but the water He would give you would become a spring within and give you eternal life. You misunderstood what He was saying and thought He meant you wouldn't have to come to this well again and be shunned by the people, and you really, really wanted that water. Then abruptly this man changed the subject. He told you to go get your husband. What did you do then?

Well, I was in a quandary. My life was so horrible that I did not want to share it with this stranger. However, I felt compelled to tell Him the truth. I had to tell Him that I did not have a husband. Would you believe He said, "That's right, you don't have a husband, but you have had five husbands, and the man you are living with now is not your husband." That really scared me. I could not believe this Jewish man knew all about my private life, so I quickly changed the subject. I did not want to discuss my private life!

You did what many unbelievers do when confronted with the gospel—you brought up a theological issue—the proper place to worship. You did not want the conversation to get personal. He knew too much about you, so you tried to direct the conversation to something else. You asked; "Where is the best place to worship: Jerusalem like the Jews do, or Mount Gerizim where the Samaritans worship?"

He would not let me change the subject. He let me know that where you worship is not the issue. Who and how you worship define true worshipers, not where you worship. He made it clear to me the religion I grew up with was wrong when He said, "You worship what you do not know, but we know what we worship because salvation comes through the Jews." I knew that He meant that only through the Jewish Messiah would the whole world, even the Samaritans like me, find salvation and worship in spirit and truth. I told Him I knew the Messiah would come someday, and when he comes, He would explain everything to us. Then He really shocked me for He said, "I am the Messiah."

Samantha, here you are a Samaritan, born and raised in a culture of pagan religion, yet you were expressing faith.

It is true maybe your faith was the size of a mustard seed, but that is all it takes. You knew enough to know that when the Messiah came He would tell you all things, so the Father must surely have been revealing the truth to you.

I just knew that as soon as I mentioned the Messiah, this man said, "I who speak to you am He." I was in shock. Here was the Messiah, the long awaited One, conversing with me, a Samaritan outcast.

This was the most recorded direct claim that Jesus ever made that He was the Messiah. I think He revealed that fact to you because you told Him that you had been looking for the Messiah. You may not have understood everything at that time, but your faith would grow, and you already had faith enough to believe He was who He said He was. He would never have revealed Himself to an unbeliever. Then Scripture tells us that the disciples came back and were not pleased to see Jesus talking to a Samaritan woman of questionable reputation.

I left because it was evident the disciples did not want me there. I left so quickly that I left my water pot there. However, it was not by accident I left it. I fully intended to come back with others from the village. I was so excited; I had met the Messiah, for heaven's sakes! I could not keep quiet. I wanted the men of the town to know that Jesus had told me everything I ever did (and my past included some of them). I was no longer trying to cover up my sin; I was forgiven and I wanted everyone to know it. In fact, as I ran, I told everyone, "The Messiah is here, come and see Him!"

Despite your reputation, many came to see Jesus. They wanted to see for themselves. They probably could see in your face and your voice that you had an incredible experience.

* * *

Samantha's statement that she had been looking for the Messiah is a reminder to us that we should be constantly looking for His coming in our day. Her response was typical of a new believer. The person who has just had the burden of sin and guilt lifted always wants to share the good news with others. Her excitement was understandable. The immediate impact of this woman's testimony on the city of Sychar was profound. Scripture tells us that many of the Samaritans of that city believed in Him because of the word of this woman. Jesus had indeed found a true worshiper. Within three years after the Samaritan woman's meeting with Christ at Jacob's well, the church was founded. Tradition tells us that the Samaritan village of Sychar became a gospel activity and witness. This woman, who began her new life by bringing many others to Christ, no doubt continued her evangelistic ministry. Only heaven will reveal the far-reaching fruits of this extraordinary woman's encounter with the Messiah.

THOUGHTS FOR DISCUSSION FROM THE LIFE OF THE WOMAN AT THE WELL

- Since most Jews did not go through Samaria on their way to Galilee, what was Jesus doing in Samaria?

- This woman was a social outcast, a Samaritan, and a woman. Why would Jesus speak to her?

- This woman was not shy about asking questions of Jesus. How do you think Jesus feels when we ask Him the hard questions? Are we ever afraid to ask the hard questions of Jesus?

- Are you ever afraid to discuss theological matters with someone because you are afraid you do not know the Bible well enough? What does God tell us to do about this?

- What did Jesus mean when He said He would give her living water?

- This woman was thirstier than she realized. What are you thirsty for spiritually?

- At what point do you think she realized they were discussing more than just well water?

- Are you uncomfortable knowing that God knows every intimate detail of your life? How does this affect how you live?

A GRATEFUL HEART
(MARY MAGDALENE)
LUKE 8:2-3, JOHN 20:1-23

Throughout Jesus' ministry, He sought to bring people into a proper relationship with God. He paid no attention to religious, social, cultural or ethnic standing. Instead, He elevated all persons to an equal position. This is probably most evident in the life of our visitor today, Mary Magdalene. Mary, you are a beautiful illustration of Christ's redemptive love. Would you tell us a little about your life?

I will be happy to do so. Even though I am Jewish, I was living in the Gentile town of Magdala, a city with a thriving fishing industry. While it is a beautiful city, located on the Sea of Galilee, it was known for its sensuality and pleasure-seeking lifestyle. Prostitution was practiced openly.

Perhaps living in the town called "the seat of prostitution" caused rumors about your lifestyle. However, it has never been corroborated you were an immoral person. Your name is mentioned fourteen times in the Gospels, however, we really know very little about you. Tell us about meeting Jesus.

I had suffered all my life with demons. When I met Jesus, He drove seven demons from my body. After being healed completely, I became a devoted follower, and joined the close circle of women who traveled with Him. We provided for Him

154

financially, and supported Him in His ministry. The disciples also traveled with us. We were careful to be separate and respectable to maintain the credibility of Jesus as a religious teacher. We were so grateful for all He had done for us. It was such a blessing to minister with Jesus.

Even though Jesus traveled with a group of women and the disciples, there was never talk of immorality. If there was such talk, the Pharisees would have accused Him of immorality, but there is no record they ever did so. After three years, the unthinkable happened – the crucifixion! You were there, along with some of the other women. I am sure you stood as close to the cross as was allowed. You had been with Jesus in His life, and now you would be close to Him as He faced death. All the disciples except John fled for fear of their lives, but you and the other women watched until the end.

We could not leave even though it broke our hearts. We felt we could not desert Him now because He had done so much for us. We stood as close to the cross as we could get, watching every dreadful action, and praying constantly for Him.

Mary, no one can even imagine what it was like for you and the other women standing there at the foot of the cross. You would not leave as long as He drew a breath. Yes, Jesus was divine, but He was also human, and He suffered. I am sure it helped knowing you and the other women were there because you loved Him. When the end finally came, you watched as they took Him down from the cross. You knew now what you had to do. You were facing what every Jewish woman has to do eventually – preparing the body of someone she loved for burial.

We wept as we watched them take His broken body from the cross. Mary and I watched and listened as Joseph of

Arimarthea asked for the body of Christ. We secretly followed him to the tomb and watched where He laid my Savior. There *was no time to prepare His body for burial, for the Sabbath was about to begin.* We determined to come back after the Sabbath to wash and anoint His body properly. *We watched as they placed Him in the tomb and rolled a stone to close the entrance.*

We know what happened next. You were up before daybreak and on your way to the tomb. When you reached the tomb, you found the stone rolled away. You ran and found Simon Peter and the disciple whom Jesus loved. You informed them someone had taken the body of Jesus and you did not know where they had put Him. Mary, you did not remember the Scriptures said He would rise from the dead.

No, I did not remember that, but I could not leave. I was standing outside the tomb crying, and someone walked up to me and asked, "Why are you crying? Who are you looking for?" I thought it was the gardener until He spoke my name. Then I recognized this was my Lord and Savior. I rushed to touch Him, but He told me not to touch Him because He had not yet ascended to His Father. You cannot imagine the joy I felt!

Mary, it was discovering the empty tomb and seeing the risen Christ that you responded to with joy and obedience. What did you do?

I did what He told me to do. He said, "Go and tell the disciples!" I ran as fast as I could and told the disciples I had seen Jesus. They did not believe me, so they ran to see for themselves. I would not have believed either if I had not seen the empty tomb. I took what Jesus said as my mandate for the rest of my life; I was to go out and tell others what Christ had done for me.

Thank you, Mary, for sharing your testimony with us. Your story is a heartwarming example of thankful living.

* * *

Jesus miraculously freed Mary's life when He drove seven demons from her body. As we heard her story, she lived out her gratitude and appreciation for the freedom Christ had given her. This freedom allowed her to stand under Christ's cross when the disciples deserted Him. After Jesus' death, she intended to give His body every respect. Like the rest of Jesus' followers, she never expected His bodily resurrection, but she was overjoyed to discover it. Her faith was genuine. She was more eager to believe and obey than to understand everything. Jesus honored her faith by appearing to her first and giving her the honor of being the first to proclaim the message of His resurrection.

THOUGHTS FOR DISCUSSION FROM THE LIFE OF MARY MAGDALENE

- Scripture tells us Mary Magdalene was one of the women who traveled with Jesus, took care of His needs, and provided for Him from her substance. What do you think that means?

- Evil spirits had tormented Mary Magdalene for years before Jesus healed her. In what way is every believer tormented prior to accepting Christ as his/her Savior?

- Even though we may not be filled with demons, we may be depressed and filled with shame and fear. Is it possible to break free of our past? How can we help others who are dealing with this kind of agony? Share an example of how you broke free of your past.

- Mary Magdalene supported Jesus with her means. Have you ever realized that you were not supporting your church as you should? How did you come to that realization?

- Do you believe that unbelievers look at you as part of Jesus' close circle of disciples? Why or why not?

- Jesus told Mary Magdalene to "go and tell." Since He gives us the same mandate, how are you fulfilling that calling?

A SINFUL WOMAN REDEEMED
(WOMAN AT SIMON THE
PHARISEE'S HOUSE)
LUKE 7:36–50

Our next guest is here to share her testimony of how she made a U-turn in her life when she met Jesus. She does not want to share her name. You will understand why when you hear her story. I am going to call her Grace.

Grace, do you mind telling us about your early life? Tell us how you became "a woman of the streets"?

I do not mind sharing my testimony because it has a happy ending. When I was born in Galilee, times were hard. I don't know exactly how or why I came to be the town prostitute. Maybe it was because I was raised by a mother who set the example before me. From a child I did not know anything else. I never knew my father, and I was labeled illegitimate from birth. I knew I had no prospects of ever being married or having a normal home life. I was the object of cutting criticism and insults by the wives of my customers. I have been spat upon and the brunt of nasty jokes. I have been shunned by the "best" people in town, and used and abused by the worst.

How sad that you had to suffer that way from a child. When I hear what you have been through, I can sense a wounded spirit with little self-esteem. However, you just knew there had to be something better. You had heard of Jesus and the miracles He had performed, and you thought He might help you. When Jesus came to dinner at the Pharisee Simon's home, you felt this was your opportunity to see Him. It was the custom of the day for all sorts of people to come hear the pearls of wisdom that fell from the visiting rabbi's lips. Today that would be considered "crashing the party," but it was allowed in those days. Tell us of your encounter with Jesus.

I was so excited when I heard that I might get to see Him. I was waiting with the others when He came in. I was able to work my way around to a place to stand directly behind Him. I was overcome with the beauty of His presence. I began to weep softly. I did not want to draw attention to myself. However, because He was reclining at the table, some of my tears fell on his feet. I could not stop crying. I was beyond caring what people thought or said. I just desperately wanted His grace and His mercy.

It is hard for us to imagine a life like yours. Your feeling that you had to see Jesus to make a change in your life indicates the Holy Spirit was drawing you. Jesus knew your heart. By now, Simon had noticed you, and I am surprised he did not throw you out.

I am sure he would have liked to throw me out, but before he could do so, I knelt and began to massage the feet of Jesus. Just sitting at the feet of the perfect Son of God, I was once again overcome with my own unworthiness and my love for Him. All I had to give Him was the precious oil I used in my trade. I took the precious oil and poured it on the feet of Jesus. I not only gave Him my only material possession; I gave Him my heart. I unbound my hair and began to wipe his feet.

I am sure you knew that letting your hair down in public was a shameful thing to do. However, at this point you were beyond caring. Then you not only wiped His feet with your hair, but you began to kiss His feet. This was not some sexual thing, as some have suggested, but in your culture kissing the feet was considered a common mark of deep reverence, especially to leading rabbis. I know as soon as you opened the bottle of perfume everyone in the room was aware of your presence. They saw you weeping, kissing, and caressing the feet of Jesus with your long black hair. I am sure everyone was shocked. Most of the guests, along with the host, knew your reputation, and I am sure they probably thought this display was downright scandalous.

Oh yes, I could tell by Simon's body language and the expression on his face that he was thinking if Jesus really was a prophet He would know it was a sinful woman touching Him. I could see he was angry with me, but I didn't care. People had judged me all my life, and now, more than I cared about what others thought, I wanted the new life Jesus offered.

Jesus did not let Simon's judgmental attitude go unchallenged. He told a parable that contrasted the Pharisees and sinners, and again the sinners came out ahead. Simon had committed several social errors in neglecting to wash Jesus' feet, anoint his head with oil, and offer him the kiss of greeting. I suppose Simon, the Pharisee, thought He was too good to treat this Jew as an equal.

Oh yes, he was very angry. However, Jesus did not linger on Simon's shortcomings. He turned, looked directly at me, and said my faith had saved me and my sins were forgiven. I'm sure the other guests didn't understand why Jesus would even speak to a sinner like me. He even wished me shalom, which means peace, prosperity, goodness, and blessings. Praise God, my life has been forever changed!

It is through God's grace that I can see in you now the beauty and glory; the countenance of one forever changed, lifted up, and loved. That must have been the best dinner party you ever attended! Isn't God good? Everyone is invited to attend such a party—one that offers grace and mercy, forgiveness and opportunity for a changed life.

THOUGHTS FOR DISCUSSION FROM
THE LIFE OF THE SINFUL WOMAN

- This woman made a bold step in going to Simon's home knowing that she would not be welcome. Were you bold when you were seeking Jesus? Did you go to someone, or did someone come to you?

- What was this woman's motive in coming to Jesus? Was she already saved? Did her salvation come out of gratitude and love, or did she come seeking to be saved? Defend your answer.

- Do you think this sinful woman would feel comfortable worshipping in your church? If not, how could you solve that problem? What would you change about your church services?

- Jesus forgave the woman of her sin just as He forgives us when we come to Him in true repentance. What do you think Jesus meant when He told her it was not her love that saved her? What did He say saved her?

- Do you initiate contact with fellow believers who may be struggling in some way, or do you wait for them to come to you? Why might some who need guidance never ask for it?

- Are you too inhibited in church services to risk worshiping Jesus the way our heart dictates because we are afraid of humiliation or what people will think? Would you like to be more emotional or outgoing in your worship but are too timid?

- There are hurting and broken people sitting in our church pews every service. Do you ignore them, or do you go out of your way to make them feel comfortable and welcome? If you found the sinful woman sitting next to you next Sunday, what would you do?

BE SURE YOUR SINS WILL
FIND YOU OUT (SAPPHIRA)
ACTS 5:1–10

Have you ever wondered what it would have been like to live during the time of Jesus' ministry and the beginning of the early church? We read in Scriptures this was a time of explosive growth for the church, and all believers were of one heart and soul. We are fortunate to have with us today a member of that early church. This is Sapphira, and she is going to tell us a little about this church.

My husband Ananias and I came into the church after Pentecost. It was a wonderful time! We shared possessions and property because of the unity brought by the Holy Spirit working in the lives of believers. That meant sharing was voluntary, and we were expected to contribute to a common treasury to meet common needs. It did not involve all private property, but only as much as was needed. It was not a membership requirement in order to be a part of the church.

Let us get this straight. No one was forced into such an agreement. Anyone could withdraw from the community if they did not want to meet the requirements of those who believed with one heart and soul. However, if you had agreed to it voluntarily, this agreement would become a sacred pledge for the faithful. Moreover, Peter had stated that it was not required of them to give up all their property. Their property still belonged to them, and they were to share voluntarily with those in need.

God blessed Ananias and me materially and we were among the more affluent members of the early Christian community. We were strongly committed to giving to those in need. We set the example of giving for others in the church. We dedicated ourselves to a certain percentage of all we had to the common good. Yes, great grace was upon our people.

Sapphira, this young church, now numbering about 5,000 was undergoing a stern test in all its responsibilities. You and Ananias had accepted the claims of the Holy Spirit on your lives and agreed to join the Christian community. You were under no obligation to sell your property, or after selling it, to give all the money to the church. Tell us what happened that caused you and Ananias to fall so quickly into sin?

I really don't know where it all began. We saw Barnabas, a good man who was full of the Holy Ghost, sell his land and bring all the money he had received and laid it at the apostles' feet. We saw how people loved and respected him. I guess we became a little jealous of the attention he was getting. We had a great deal of property to sell, and Ananias and I discussed withdrawing from the community of believers so we would not have to give the amount of money we had agreed to give. However, Ananias did not want to leave the community because he enjoyed the position he held. We discussed all the things the money could buy. We finally decided if we did not tell the community of believers how much we made from the sale of the property, no one would know we were not giving our pledge.

You mean you agreed to lie about the money. Greed has been the downfall of many people down through the ages.

Sapphira, God has blessed women with the unique power of influence. A wife cannot always influence her husband to do right, but she can try. I am surprised you did not try to talk your husband out of this dishonest scheme. We do not have record that you tried to influence your husband to do the right thing.

That is the reason I was eager to talk with you today. I want to warn women to be careful how you influence your husband. I did not try to talk Ananias out of the plan to keep some of the money from the sale of our property for ourselves. I have to confess I encouraged him to lie. I thought no one would know. The consequences are not worth it! You know the rest of the story. When Ananias handed Peter the money from the sale of our property, Peter knew instantly he was lying. At that moment, Ananias dropped dead.

* * *

Now for the rest of the story. Sapphira did not know her husband had dropped dead, so she came a few hours later with the same lie they had agreed to tell the brethren. Do you suppose that if she had known her husband was dead, she would have lied? Sapphira's greatest sin as a member of this early band of Christians was not that she and her husband withheld a part of the proceeds from the sale of their land, but that they lied to the Holy Spirit. When Sapphira and her husband came into the church and laid this money from the sale of the land at the apostle's feet, they were pretending to be something they were not. In the eyes of the people, they appeared generous; but in the eyes of God, they were hypocrites. They wanted more than just being members of the body. They wanted the praise of men.

THOUGHTS FOR DISCUSSION
FROM THE LIFE OF SAPPHIRA

- What excuses might Sapphira and Ananias have given themselves for lying to the church? Do you ever use some of the same excuses?

- If they truly needed the money they held back, what options did they have instead of lying to the church?

- Do you think Sapphira's problem was jealousy of the recognition Barnabas received for his giving?

- Why did Ananias and Sapphira come alone to present their gifts to Peter instead of coming as a couple? Could it be because we all stand alone before the judgment of God? Discuss.

- How might Sapphira's story have ended differently if she and her husband had submitted to the Lordship of Christ in their marriage?

- Ananias and Sapphira were the first hypocrites in the early church. Others through the ages have lied to God and not been punished with death. Why do you think God punished Ananias and Sapphira with death?

- When you make a commitment to God or your church, are you careful to keep your commitment?

GOD'S JOYFUL MAID (RHODA)
ACTS 12:12–17

We are fortunate to have with us today a young woman who played a big part in the growth of the early Christian church. Welcome Rhoda, what would you like us to know about you?

I have to tell you, I love serving the Lord. I am proud to say that I am a servant girl in the home of Mary, the mother of John Mark. Since I am a servant, you might say I have no life of my own; however, I love my job. Mary is a good Christian woman and she treats me like a daughter. Her home is always open for Christian prayer meetings and get-togethers. During out times together, we pray especially for the disciples and others who are undergoing such persecution at this time. By watching these older Christians, I have learned to praise the Lord with joy and thanksgiving. I love being a part of these prayer meetings

Rhoda, I would guess all the entertaining makes your job harder because you have to work long hours some days. Do you resent the extra hours you have to spend serving and cleaning?

Oh my, no. I count it a blessing. I love it because I get to hang around with all these wonderful Christian people. I have learned so much from them. I am always amazed at their joyful attitude, no matter what the circumstance. They are not just happy; they are downright joyful! Mary says there is a difference in happiness and joy. She says happiness depends on circumstances, and circumstances change, but joy depends on God, and God never changes. I have determined I will have joy in my life.

That is amazing for one so young who has spent her time waiting on other people. We know you lived in the time of religious persecution. In fact, the group meeting at this house received an awful shock when you heard that John's brother James was beheaded for preaching the good news.

We recently had a prayer meeting about that very thing. We trusted our God to protect us, even unto death if that was His will for our lives. Our joy is in the Lord, and we do not fear those who can kill our bodies. We had heard they had taken Peter off to prison and planned to kill him when the Passover ended. Herod knew that would please the Pharisees and priests. We knew we had to pray for Peter. He was our leader, and we depended on him.

There is nothing like trouble to make people pray. I understand a message was sent to all Christians, inviting them to a prayer meeting at Mary's house. That prayer meeting lasted all night. Things did not look good for Peter.

No, the outlook was not good. This prayer meeting took place on the last day of the Passover. We knew Peter's trial would begin the next day and he would probably be executed. We gathered for an all-night prayer meeting and began praying earnestly. I was getting a little weary about midnight when I heard a knock at the door. That made me wide-awake. I knew as the maid I was expected to see who was there.

I can imagine how frightened you were. You probably wondered if it could be soldiers coming to take you all away.

However, you opened the grille to see who was there. Were you surprised?

Surprised is an understatement! When I saw who was standing there, I slammed the grille shut, and ran as fast as I could to tell the others Peter was at the door. They looked at me as if they thought I was mad! They did not believe me. I heard one of them say, "Don't pay any attention to her, she's just a dumb blonde!" Another one said, "Peter can't be there; he's in jail, chained between two soldiers, with more soldiers keeping guard." However, I knew what I saw. Peter just kept knocking, so I tried to make them understand. "I know it is Peter and we must let him in!" I said as I led the way and opened the door. We were overjoyed to see Peter there. I could not help saying, "I told you so." It was a wonderful moment.

Isn't that just like Christians? We pray and then we are surprised to have an answer. It is almost as if we did not believe our God was going to answer anyway. What a wonderful prayer meeting that must have been as you all listened to Peter tell how his escape took place.

Peter told how God had sent His angel to wake him as he lay sleeping. When the angel told him to stand up, his handcuffs fell off. Peter thought he was dreaming when the angel told him to put on his clothes. Then the angel brought him through two guard posts unnoticed. They came to the outer gate and it just opened by itself. Peter said he hurried to Mary's house because he knew we would be there praying for him. Then he looked directly at me, and said, "I had been though all that, and this little lady left me standing at the door!" I could not say why I did it, except I was overcome with joy that our prayers had been answered, and I wanted everyone to know. How could I keep quiet with such wonderful news?

We should all ask that question ourselves about the spreading of the gospel. How can we keep quiet when we have such a wonderful message to share? Isn't it wonderful that Peter knew his friends would be praying for him? That is what Christian friends do!

THOUGHTS FOR DISCUSSION
FROM THE LIFE OF RHODA

- What was Rhoda's life like as a slave girl? What made her life joyful?

- What had Rhoda learned about the difference in happiness and joy?

- Are you joyful in your work for the Lord? Why or why not? What changes need to be made in order for you to serve the Lord with joy?

- As Rhoda and the others prayed for Peter's release from prison, do you think they were doubtful he would be released? Give reasons supporting your view.

- When Rhoda shut the door in Peter's face, do you think it was because she did not believe it was he, or did she slam the door out of excitement?

- The ones praying dismissed the servant girl as being a little crazy. What is your opinion of Rhoda?

- Do you begin to doubt God when He does not answer your prayers on your timetable?

- Do you pray in faith that God will answer your prayer if you pray in His will? Can you quote a scripture that tells us to pray believing?

A WOMAN WITH A LOVING AND GIVING HEART (DORCAS)
ACTS 9:36-42

Scripture describes our next guest this way, "This woman was full of good works and charitable deeds which she did." Welcome Dorcas. We are thrilled to have you with us today, and we are anxious to hear your story. But first, tell us a little about yourself.

I was born and raised in Joppa, a city located about 40 miles west of Jerusalem along the beautiful Mediterranean coast in Israel. Those in the Greek culture called me Dorcas, but the Aramaic name given to me at birth was Tabitha. I was named for the gazelle, a small, swift animal that symbolized beauty in the Middle East. I was saved when Philip the evangelist came to Joppa preaching the message of forgiveness and redemption for the Gentiles as well as for the Jews. It was an exciting time in my hometown of Joppa! We were one of the earliest cities to have a Christian population.

Dorcas, you were known as a believer and for your good works. Tell us how you became interested in doing the good works we read about.

Philip had been a deacon in the church at Jerusalem and he shared their concern for the widows and those unable to care for themselves. His messages challenged us to seek what it was that God would have us do. I couldn't do much, but I could sew. I had watched the fatherless children, the poverty stricken widows, the sick, and the aged wandering up and down the coast without proper clothing. It broke my heart, and God seemed to be calling me to do something. I began by inviting the ladies in the town to a sewing circle in my home. We made tunics, cloaks, and children's clothing. It was amazing to see the transformation when these people, once clothed in rags, go away renewed in spirit in their new, well-fitting garments. That was my ministry.

And what a wonderful ministry it was, and how the people must have loved you. You stitched layettes for babies, made cloaks, robes, sandals, and other apparel for poverty-stricken widows, the sick and aged. This continual service to the needy not only speaks of a giving heart but a woman of great faith. How the people of the town must have loved and depended on you. But something happened to you. Can you tell us about that?

I will be glad to tell you what a great God we serve. I contracted an illness that was always fatal back then. I can't remember all that happened but I just know that I was told later that my illness did lead to my death. I was told that the saints in the Church and the widows I had befriended made their way to my house, washed me and laid me in the upper room, the very room where we had made garments. And knowing some of these ladies whom I loved, I'm sure they stood around weeping as they planned my burial. Even though we had heard Peter preach about raising people from the dead, these ladies had little faith that I could be brought back from the dead.

But God had other plans, didn't He? Peter happened to be preaching about 10 miles away in a little town called

Lydda. Because you were much loved and respected, the disciples sent two men to ask Peter to come without delay. They had heard that Peter had performed miracles and this rough, salty seaman believed he could raise this good Christian woman from the dead. Peter came immediately and went upstairs where they had laid you. All the widows stood around him, crying and showing him the robes and other clothing you had made while you were still with them. Peter sent them all out of the room; then he got down on his knees and prayed. Then he held out his hand to you and said, "Tabitha, get up." Tell us what happened then.

I opened my eyes, and seeing Peter I sat up. Peter took me by the hand and helped me to my feet. Then he called the believers and widows and said, "Here she is to continue her walk with you. God has healed her because of her faith." I was amazed and found it hard to comprehend all that was happening. God had chosen me to display His power through healing. I was overwhelmed, as were my friends, and you can imagine the good time we had weeping, shouting, and praising God for His goodness and mercy to me.

That must have been some prayer meeting. I'm sure the shouts of praise and gratitude to God were louder than the wails at your death had been. The people whom you had befriended were filled with a joy that only those who see the dead restored to life can experience. And you, Dorcas, the woman who had lifted up so many in body and spirit, had now been lifted up yourself. Scriptures tell us that because so many people had seen the miracle, many came to faith in Him. Several times in the New Testament, God uses miracles when He wants to authenticate the message of salvation, but here in Joppa, He was using your healing to show the world His truth about which He is, the all powerful One who controls all life.

* * *

The example set by Dorcas all those years ago is everlasting. Many women throughout history have sought to emulate her life by establishing Dorcas societies that hold humanitarian activities to help others. There are Dorcas societies today in many of our churches. Their mandate is James 1:27 which says, "Religion that God our Father accepts as pure and faultless is this: to look after orphans and widows in their distress and to keep oneself from being polluted by the world." Our good works testify about faith and prove that we are believers.

THOUGHTS FOR DISCUSSION
FROM THE LIFE OF DORCAS

- Dorcas' story teaches us that God can use all people no matter how small or large the gift. Have you discovered your gift?

- Share a time in your life when God opened or closed a door thereby giving you the opportunity to discover your spiritual gift?

- Are you ever jealous of someone else's spiritual gift? Instead of wishing for something you don't have, why not make good use of the gifts God has given you?

- What seemingly insignificant talent or ability do you possess that would mean a great deal to someone in need? Are you using that talent?

- Does your church have a ministry of helping fatherless children, poverty stricken widows, sick and aged? Have you thought about starting a sewing circle?

- What are some of the reasons we give for not doing good works? Do you dare question yourself as to whether they are valid reasons or excuses?

- What fruit of the spirit would you say Dorcas possessed?

- What fruit of the spirit do you possess?

A WOMAN WITH THE RIGHT
PRIORITIES (LYDIA)
ACTS 16:13–15

Today, I would like you to meet an extraordinary woman. Her name is Lydia, and we know little about her, except she ran a purple dye business. Let us see if we can find out a little more about this woman and her unusual business. Lydia, will you tell us where you conducted your business?

I was from Thyatira, but chose to conduct my business in Philippi. Philippi is on the eastern Macedonia great east-west highway between Rome and Asia. This location made for a more lucrative enterprise.

Lydia, we know you were a dealer in purple cloth. Where did you get the purple dye, and who were your customers?

At this time, there were two types of purple cloth available. The most expensive cloth was made from a shellfish known as the murex. The murex is a tropical sea snail that excretes a yellow fluid. When this fluid is exposed to sunlight, it becomes a purple dye. The Tyrian dye made from the murex was one of the most precious of all commodities in the ancient world. My customers included imperial families and Babylonian buyers who bought purple for temple curtains.

Lydia, as a very successful businesswoman, you certainly must have had to balance many priorities in your life. While you worked full time as a merchant, you also had a significant ministry with the women in Philippi. You met regularly with women who gathered to pray on the Sabbath. Apparently, this small group of women was the only public gathering of Jews anywhere in Philippi. Luke describes you as a woman who worshiped God, even though you had not yet become a convert to Judaism. You were a Gentile, but your heart was open. You were a seeker before you heard the message that changed your life. God was already drawing you.

Yes, I was seeking. I knew something was missing in my life. I began meeting with some other women who felt the same way. We met on the riverbank at Philippi every Sunday morning to worship together. The banks of that river offered peace and quiet away from the populous hill section of the city. We met because we longed to know more about one true God. We prayed for guidance and understanding.

Then one day God answered your prayers. Unbeknownst to you, the providential guidance from God was becoming evident to the Apostle Paul and his companions. Scripture tells us Paul had planned to go to Asia, but had been forbidden by the Spirit of God to go to Asia Minor. While waiting for God's guidance, Paul received a revelation calling him to Macedonia to preach the gospel. Was God calling Him in answer to the prayers of this little group of women in Macedonia? Lydia, tell us what happened.

The women and I were at the riverbank praying when we saw two men coming toward us. We were startled at first, because men had never joined us. They sat down and began to speak to us. We could see instantly that there was something different about these men. They explained this was the apostle Paul, and he had been given a vision from the Lord he was to come to Macedonia. We had asked for guidance, and now God had sent this man and his companions to teach us what we needed to know. We became excited as Paul related the story of the new gospel of Jesus Christ being proclaimed in Jerusalem.

Lydia, I cannot help but think what keen foresight and courage it took on your part to accept the story of this new gospel. Did you ever think embracing this new gospel might affect your business? I am sure some of your customers would probably have scoffed at the gospel of Christ.

All I could think of was the message I was hearing that salvation was free! I did not have to work for my salvation; it was a gift from God. I never thought of the customers I might lose.

God's sovereign hand can be seen clearly in every aspect of your story. The Lord clearly orchestrated the circumstances that brought Paul to Macedonia, and you were waiting with a seeking heart. The Spirit of God opened your heart and caused you to embrace the truth of the gospel, and become a believer. You immediately felt the need to be baptized. Lydia, will you share with us why the urgency to be baptized.

I asked to be baptized as soon as possible because I wanted to be obedient to my Lord. It was my first opportunity to witness publicly for my Lord. Since we were on the riverbank already, I was baptized immediately. Because of my public confession of faith, my whole family accepted Christ. They were also baptized.

Lydia, how wonderful! You were a new Christian, and you were already winning people to the Lord. In addition, you were quick to show hospitality to the missionaries. Paul and his companions stayed with you during their time in Macedonia. I am sure you knew the danger of housing these strangers.

I knew the local Jews would hold me responsible, and I might lose some of my business. I also knew the community might look down on me for having Paul and his team at my home. However, I wanted them to stay and teach us this good news. In addition, it gave Paul's team a base to preach the gospel in that area. Eventually the gospel was able to penetrate all of Europe. With their help and guidance, we were able to start a church in Philippi and no longer had to meet on the riverbank. Many people were won to the Lord. Sometime after Paul and his friends left my home, I received a letter from him, which stated, "I thank my God every time I remember you. I always pray with joy because of your partnership in the gospel from the first day until now." It was an encouraging message to the struggling churches in Macedonia from the Apostle Paul.

Lydia, you have the distinction of being the first convert and the first person to be baptized in Philippi. You are known for your hospitality that was as remarkable as your faith. I can just hear you rejoicing and gaining strength as you read Paul words in Philippians 4:13, "I can do all things through Christ who strengthened me." You proved that in your own life. Christians will always remember you as the woman who picked up the first torch from Paul at Philippi and carried it steadfastly. Your reward in heaven will surely be great.

* * *

Lydia's life is our example of one who had the right priorities. She managed a successful business, led the women in prayer, and opened her home to the missionaries. The first church in Philippi met in her home, and she was a soul winner. Lydia was a role model for women in her day, and in ours.

THOUGHTS FOR DISCUSSION
FROM THE LIFE OF LYDIA

- Describe the circumstances that placed Paul in Philippi at the time Lydia became a believer. Do you believe he was there by accident?

- Share the circumstances God had arranged at the time you became a Christian.

- Give reasons why you believe God was already calling Lydia before Paul came to Philippi.

- In what ways might God use a businessperson like Lydia for spreading the gospel?

- In what ways might God be calling you to use your connections in your business to share the gospel of Jesus Christ?

- Have your priorities changed since you became a Christian? Are there priorities in your life that need to be changed as you seek to know God in a greater way?

- What is the importance of baptism after a person has accepted Jesus as Savior?

- Read Acts 16:13-15 and build a profile of Lydia.

A CAPABLE AND DEDICATED
WORKER (PRISCILLA)
ACTS 18:1–3; 24–26

Some married couples know how to make the most of life. They complement each other, capitalize on each other's strengths, and form an effective team. Their united efforts affect those around them. Aquila and Priscilla was such a couple. We never heard of them apart; however, today we have persuaded Priscilla to come answer some questions for us. Priscilla, I understand you and your husband were from Italy but were residing in Corinth.

At the time our story began, we were living in Corinth. We had left our home in Rome when Claudius, the Emperor, expelled all the Jews. We came and made our home here in Corinth because it was the political and commercial center of Greece. My husband and I both worked as tentmakers, and we lived in the weaving sections of Corinth. Being a tentmaker is not an easy job; however, we loved what we were doing, and we were able to work together. Corinth was a very wicked city. We were believing Jews, and our home became a rendezvous for those wanting to know more about the new faith. In fact, the local church met at our home regularly. •

You are an amazing woman, Priscilla. You managed your household, weaved cloth, and helped your husband make tents. In addition to being a skillful tentmaker, you were known throughout the early church community as a dedicated and influential woman. I am sure that was not an easy task. People in Corinth were beginning to worship Aphrodite, the pagan god of love and war. They were worshipping the pagan god by giving money to the temple and taking part in sexual acts with male and female Temple prostitutes. You must have been very excited when you heard Paul was coming to visit Corinth.

Yes, Aquila and I were very excited when we heard of Paul's visit. We knew he was a tentmaker by trade, so we invited him to stay with us. Paul was not afraid to confront people about their sin, and presented the gospel at every opportunity. In addition, he assisted us in cutting and sewing the woven cloth of goats' hair into tents that were used to house Roman soldiers. We received many blessings working with Paul and listening to his great teaching.

Scripture tells us Paul stayed in Corinth for the next year and a half teaching the word of God. Eventually, he was charged with promoting a religion not approved by Roman law. This charge amounted to treason. Paul was not encouraging obedience to a human king other than Caesar, nor was he speaking against the Roman Empire. He only spoke about Christ's eternal kingdom.

The Roman Empire recognized religion only under Roman law. As long as Christians were seen as part of Judaism, there was not a problem. However, because Christianity was not part of Judaism, some Jews began to cause trouble. When Paul left Cornith, he invited Aquila and me to go with him. We settled in Ephesus, and Paul went on to do the work God had called him to do. Aquila and I stayed in Ephesus and continued the work Paul had started there. Again, we opened our home to the church, and passed along to new Christians the things Paul taught us.

I know many were won to the Lord because of the warm place to worship and the learning you provided in your home. You and Aquila were a great evangelistic team for the Lord. In an age where the focus seems mostly on what happens between a husband and wife, you and Aquila are examples of what can happen through a husband and wife working together in God's will. Priscilla, I understand you had another young preacher come to Ephesus, and you invited him to stay in your home.

Shortly after Paul left, a young man named Apollos came to Ephesus. We were very impressed with his amazing natural talent for public speaking. The people loved him and listened with great admiration. Apollos spoke boldly in public, and was interpreting and applying Old Testament Scriptures effectively. He debated opponents of Christianity forcefully and effectively. However, it was not long before we realized he did not have the whole story. His preaching was based on the Old Testament and John the Baptist's message. Aquila and I decided we had to set the young man straight.

That must have been hard to do, but you understood that effective communication of the gospel includes an accurate message delivered with God's power. Some of the Ephesians were beginning to follow Apollos instead of his message. You were wise to realize Apollos' limited knowledge could hurt the cause of Christ. You were determined this young preacher would be a well-informed, inspiring proponent of the gospel. How did he accept your correction?

Although his natural abilities could have made him proud, as many young preachers would have been, Apollos was eager to learn. We shared with him all Paul taught us. We pointed out he had only been preaching the first step of salvation. The whole message is to repent from sin and turn to belief in Christ. We shared with Apollos the life, death, and resurrection of Jesus. We introduced him to the teaching of the Holy Spirit's place in our lives. We shared how, after we are saved, the Holy Spirit dwells in our heart, empowering us to do God's will. As we talked with him, we could see scripture he already knew becoming clearer to him. He thanked us for helping him to see the whole picture of salvation. His preaching became filled with new energy and boldness.

What a wonderful story. You were just passing along what you and Aquila had learned from sitting under the teachings of Paul. Because Apollos did not hesitate to be a student, he probably became a better teacher. I want to mention again what great evangelists you and Aquila were. Your effectiveness as a team is a result of your good relationship with each other. The Christian home is still one of the best tools for spreading the gospel. Your hospitality opened the doorway of salvation to many in Corinth and Ephesus. What a lesson to us who spend our time bickering or finding fault, when we should be proclaiming the gospel and/or mentoring those who are less knowledgeable of the scriptures.

THOUGHTS FOR DISCUSSION
FROM THE LIFE OF PRISCILLA

- Do you think married couples can have an effective ministry together? Why or why not?

- Can a woman have a career in addition to being a wife and mother? Give arguments to support your view. What are the obstacles encountered?

- Do you agree the home should be a valuable tool for evangelism? Why or why not?

- Are you hospitable in inviting ministry workers to your home? What are the dangers and blessings?

- Priscilla and Aquila had opportunity to mentor the young Apollos and help him come to a proper understanding of the good news. Do you have sufficient knowledge of the scriptures to mentor someone? Tell of a time you have mentored someone.

- Apollos received correction from Aquila and Priscilla with a heart willing to learn. How could the situation have turned out differently? How do you feel when someone points out your mistakes?

- Priscilla was a competent worker with her husband in the tent making business. How could their competence in the workplace be a positive witness for Christ?

TRAIN UP A CHILD
(EUNICE AND LOIS)
2 TIMOTHY 1:3-6 Acts 16:1

In an age of negative influences bombarding children from all sides, we are fortunate to have with us today a mother and grandmother who can be examples to us as we raise our children and grandchildren. I would like to introduce you to Eunice, mother of Timothy, and Lois, his grandmother. Eunice, let us begin with you. Will you tell us a little about yourself?

My mother and I live in Lystra, a city in the Roman Province of Galatia, and that is where my son Timothy was born and raised. I am Jewish, but Timothy's father was Greek. How I came to marry a Greek is another story, which I won't go into at this time. He is no longer with us, so I have had to raise Timothy by myself.

Eunice, you couldn't get on the phone and call Doctor Spock or Doctor Laura for advice, so you turned to your mother for advice on how to raise your son. What would we do without mothers? I am sure Lois was a great help to you. She had taught you scripture, and you were determined to do the same for your son. It was because of your dedication to spiritual instruction that Timothy became a godly man and faithful disciple of Christ.

The scripture that I claimed for my son was Proverbs 22:6, "Train up a child in the way he should go, and when he is old he will not depart from it." Timothy was an obedient child and was always eager to learn scriptures and Bible stories. I loved finding unique and unusual ways of teaching him scriptures, and we had fun studying and learning together. I believed it was my duty as a mother to teach my son scripture. I tried to make an application for every incident in my Timothy's young life. For instance, when his little dog gave its life protecting Timothy from a dangerous animal, it was the perfect opportunity to tell how Christ had given up His life for us. I enjoyed teaching and learning with my son. As a single mother, I had to work to support my son and mother, but I was fortunate to have my mother to take care of Timothy. It was a comfort knowing she would continue to help Timothy grow in his faith.

Eunice, mothers like you face the daily challenges of parenting, and it must be especially hard to have to leave him every day and go to work. However, such a mother will reap abundant rewards by having a loving relationship with her child, and a loving grandmother such as Lois.

Lois, will you tell us how you were used by God to help nurture this young man?

I just prayed for my grandson, as I had prayed for his mother. I talked of our faith, and encouraged him to memorize scripture. We talked about salvation in Jesus Christ. How that child could ask questions! I taught him a simple prayer until he was old enough to form his own prayers. I regularly reminded him of the awesome power of God to face life's challenges. We explored the meaning of the scriptures and studied Jewish traditions. Timothy loved the exciting stories of the Old Testament scriptures. I taught him to sing the Psalms, and we talked of the choices he would someday have to make. Timothy always knew his mother and I were praying for him daily.

What an awesome grandmother you were Lois, and what an example to grandmothers today. I am sure you prepared him well for going forth with Paul and Silas to preach the gospel. We can imagine the sadness you both experienced as you bid your beloved Timothy goodbye.

We were sad, but like Hannah of old, when she left her young Samuel in the House of the Lord, we could overcome our earthly affection for Timothy, and say as Hannah did, "We have lent him to the Lord; as long as he liveth he shall be lent to the Lord."

Eunice and Lois, you gave up your child willingly and without reservation to the cause of Christ. The Apostle Paul called Timothy, "my beloved son." Only the early training Timothy received could earn this fond term from the childless and wifeless Paul.

THOUGHTS FOR DISCUSSION FROM
THE LIVES OF EUNICE AND LOIS

- What are the dangers involved in trying to raise a child when the father or mother is of a different race or faith?

- Eunice was fortunate to have Timothy's grandmother Lois, to help her raise him. What part did your grandmother play in your life?

- What are some of the challenges that we face in raising our children today?

- Timothy's mother and grandmother provided a firm foundation for him. How are building a firm foundation for your children? Are you helping them memorize scripture and talk with them about the meaning? Do you attend church regularly? Is your life an example your children can follow?

- Is it the church's full responsibly to teach scripture to children? What is the parent's responsibility?

- What promise does God give to mothers and grandmothers who nurture their children in the faith?

- Do you often thank God for the privilege of nurturing your children to faith in Him?

Opal Ashenbrenner is a well-known Bible teacher, author and speaker. While serving as Singles Director for Southern Hills Baptist Church, Opal saw great growth in the ministry, authored dramas for her group to present, and became a consultant for the Sunday School Board of the Southern Baptist Convention and a contributor to the "Christian Singles" magazine. She has traveled throughout the nation conducting conferences, retreats and workshops, including a Divorce Recovery Workshop she wrote. She has authored two books and contributed to many publications. Opal, a widow and retired FAA employee, is in her 64th year as a Sunday School teacher and continues to lead home Bible studies and write for Christian publications. She has two wonderful children, Susie and Paul, and a precious stepdaughter, Stacy. Known as "Granapple" to her four grandchildren and two step-grandchildren, Opal counts her family as one of her greatest blessings. Opal may be reached at dgol123@sbcglobal.net.

Made in the USA
San Bernardino, CA
05 March 2017